ANUNNAKI ULEMA TECHNIQUES AND TAROT DECK TO SEE YOUR FUTURE

The world's most powerful book
on the occult, oracles and
divination
9th Edition

Introduction by Ulema Mordachai ben Zvi
Notes and Commentaries by Ulema Bukhtiar
Epilogue by Ulema Kira Yerma

TIMES SQUARE PRESS

Cover of Part 2

Maximillien de Lafayette

Anunnaki Ulema Techniques and Tarot Deck To See Your Future

The world's most powerful book on the occult and foreseeing your future on Earth and in other dimensions.

9th Edition
Previously published under
Ulema Anunnaki Tarot

Revised and Expanded

A set of 2 Parts
PART 1

***   ***   ***

Maximillien de Lafayette's books are available in 2 formats:
1-Amazon Kindle edition at www.amazon.com
2-In paperback at www.lulu.com
http://stores.lulu.com/maximilliendelafayette

Author's website:
www.maximilliendelafayettebibliography.com

Date of Publication: August 31, 2011.
Printed in the United States of America.

Maximillien de Lafayette

Anunnaki Ulema Techniques and Tarot Deck To See Your Future
PART 1
The world's most powerful book on the occult and foreseeing your future on Earth and in other dimensions.

Introduction by
Ulema Mordachai ben Zvi

Notes and Commentaries by
Ulema Bukhtiar

Epilogue by
Ulema Kira Yerma

Created by WJNA, Incorporated

***   ***   ***

9th Edition
Revised and Expanded

Jamiyat Ramadosh Al-Ulema Al-Anunnaki
London New York Paris Marseille Benares Cairo Alexandria Baalbeck
Damascus Tokyo

2011

Recommended Books

1.Expanded & revised: Description and Explanation of the Most Important Anunnaki, Babylonian, Sumerian, Akkadian, Assyrian, Phoenician Slabs, Seals, Inscriptions, Statues, Tablets and Secret Symbols
Illustrated History of the Civilizations, Religions, Folklore, and Myths of the Middle East, Near East, and Asia Minor.

2.The Revised, Expanded and Complete Series: Anunnaki and Ulema Explain the Greatest Mysteries of all Time, from 460,000 B.C. to the Present Day. (3 Volumes)
How They Created us Genetically, Life After Death, Time-Space Travel, Parallel Dimensions, UFOs, Extraterrestrials, Occult and Religions.

3.Mind-Bending Black Operations, Weapons Systems and Experiments by Extraterrestrials, Grays and Governments
The Hidden World of the Anunnaki, Ulema, Grays and Secret Military-Aliens Bases and Laboratories on Earth, Underwater and in Space

4.The Complete and Expanded book of Ramadosh:
7,000 Year Old Anunnaki Ulema Techniques To Live Longer, Happier, Healthier, Wealthier.

5.The Revised, Indexed and Complete Book of the Anunnaki-Ulema Final Warning to Humanity, the End of Time, and the Return of the Anunnaki in 2022.
The Grays' creation of a hybrid-human race, and the final clash between extraterrestrials and Earth.

6.Universal Encyclopedia of Anunnaki, Ulema, Ascended Masters and Extraterrestrial Offspring on Earth:
Everything you wanted to know about the Anunnaki and the genetic creation of Man, and our origin from the beginning of time to the present. Vol.1 (A set of 7 volumes)

*** *** ***

⌘ Table of Contents ⌘

❁❁❁

Placing the letters of your name under each corresponding letter in the Anakh/Proto-Ugaritic...67

❁❁❁

The best time to read your future...71

❁❁❁

The Tarot deck...77

❁❁❁

Pronunciation of letters and symbols...87

⌘⌘⌘

Ramiyah: The line-up of the cards...95

⌘⌘⌘

The meaning of each card...101

⌘⌘⌘

The Five Adjacent Cards...163

⌘⌘⌘

<u>Table of Contents of Part 2</u>

⌘⌘⌘

⌘⌘⌘

⌘ ⌘ ⌘

Epilogue by Ulema Kira Yerma

⌘ ⌘ ⌘

Addendum

Important information and additional guidance for reading your Bakht.

Index

19

⌘ Introduction ⌘
⌘

Bakht Kiraat is the study and reading of one's future on Earth and in other dimensions. It regroups the past into the present, and transcends the frontiers of the present to reach the realm of the future. The "Ulema Anunnaki Tarot: Lessons and Techniques to See your Future" is the first published work on Bakht. There is no other book written on the subject.

⌘ ⌘ ⌘

Bakht has been practiced by the Ulema Anunnaki for thousands of years.

It is totally unknown in the Western hemisphere.

Essentially, Bakht is based upon knowledge received from the early remnants of the Anna.Ki, also called Anu.Na.Ki, an extra-terrestrial race which landed on Earth hundreds of thousands of years ago.

Very few seers and mystics outside the circle of the Ulema Anunnaki penetrated the secrets of the Bakht. They were the elite of the priests of Ra, the early Sinhar Khaldi (Early Chaldean priests/astrologers/astronomers), the Tahar (Early Phoenician Purification priests), and the Rouhaniyiin, known in the West as the alchemists/Kabalists.

In the whole world today, there are no more 700 persons who practice the Bakht, and they are called Ba-khaat or Bakhaati. Two hundred of them are the supreme enlightened masters, called Mounawariin. The other five hundred masters are simply called Ulema Anunnaki. The teachers of the Ba-khaat or Bakhaati are called Tahiriim and the Ulema refer to them as the Baal-Shamroutiim.

Passages from the Ulema Anunnaki ancient and modern scrolls have mentioned the names of few Western/Eastern masters who have studied and practiced the Bakht, to name a few:

Alain Cardec
Archamides
Avraham ben Shmuel Abulafia
Comte de Saint Germain
Galiostro
Hakadosh Alshich
Kira Yerma
Nicholas Flammel
Pythagoras
Rabbi Loeb
Sahib Baba
Shlomo Halevi Alkabetz
Sophocles

The scrolls also included the names of the Anunnaki Sinhars who taught the Ulema, the art and science of reading the Bakht, to name a few:

Aa-kim-lu
Abekir
Abharu-Ak-Sha
Anah-Taba.Ru "Anda-Barikha"
Dadosh-Anamesch
Sinharabraach

22

Bakht is an Ana'kh word which means many things, such as fortune, fortune-telling, reading the future, luck (Bad or good), foreseeing particular segments from future events, and reading what was written in the book of your life, at the time you were born, and even before you existed on Earth.

Thousands of years later, Arab and Pre-Islamic scholars began to use the Anakh word Bakht in their Arabic language. Today, you will find the word Bakht in written and spoken Arabic.

The modern Egyptians use the word Bakht quite frequently. But the meaning has changed a little bit, because Bakht in Arabic means "Haz", and "Haz" means luck. Some fortune-tellers in Egypt and the Near East interpret "Haz" as the future.

Thus "Reading the Bakht" in Arabic today means: Foretelling your future and luck.

⌘⌘⌘

The earliest manuscript on Bakht appeared in Phoenicia, circa 7,500 B.C., and it was written in Ana'kh. A later version in Anakh-Proto-Ugaritic appeared three thousand years later. A third version written in the early Phoenician-Byblos script appeared in Byblos and Tyre.

There are also two versions in Akkadian and Old Babylonian language, which are assumed lost.

Around 65 A.D., a new version in Arabic appeared in the Arabian Peninsula, and Persia, and it was called "Firasa".
Around 685 A.D., a revised edition appeared in Damascus, Syria. It was said that, from this Syrian edition, derived the hand-written manuscript "Ilmu Al Donia" (Science or Knowledge of the Universe). This manuscript included chapters on Arwah (Spirits and non-human entities), Djins, and Afrit.

Around 1365 A.D., a book titled "Shams Al Maaref Al Koubra" appeared in Cairo and Damascus, based upon two books "Al Bakht: Dirasat Al Moustakbal", and "Ilmu Al Donia".

The book you are currently reading is based upon the first and second versions of the Ugaritic-Phoenician book of Bakht, and was originally translated, re-written/edited, and expanded upon in the mid-sixties, by Maximillien de Lafayette.

⌘ ⌘ ⌘

In the sixties, an attempt was made to publish de Lafayette's book, but leading figures from the Ulema Anunnaki circle objected very strongly. The honorable Cheik Al Baydani stated that knowledge given to the unworthy and to the un-righteous ones would produce catastrophic results. Many masters agreed.

Twenty years later, honorable Master Li authorized the release of de Lafayette's book after a rigorous review of the book, and accentuated editing of its contents were completed in 1986. The book you are currently reading is the original work of Master de Lafayette.

However, many of the original Bakht techniques that appeared in the first draft are not included in this book. Nevertheless, de Lafayette's work remains extremely useful and enlightening. The original draft consisted of 725 pages.

Honorable Master Ben Yacob and Ulema Kira Yerma decided that de Lafayette's manuscript should be finally published in the West. And I do welcome this decision.

Mordachai ben Zvi

⌘How to Use this Book⌘
⌘

- ❖ Learning the terminology:
- ❖ 2. How many pages should you read at one time?
- ❖ 3. Keep a notebook handy
- ❖ 4. More questions and unfound answers.
- ❖ 5. Cutting out the card pages from this book.
- ❖ 6. Where and how to store your cards.

⌘How to Use this Book⌘
⌘

Learning the terminology:
How many pages should you read at one time?
3. Keep a notebook handy
4. More questions and unfound answers.
5. Cutting out the card pages from this book.
6. Where and how to store your cards.

This is not an easy book.
The subject is quite complicated.
To benefit from this book, the reader is advised to take into consideration, the following:

1. Learning the terminology:

First of all, you must familiarize yourself with the Anakh, Ulemite, Proto-Ugaritic, Phoenician, Akkadian, and Old Babylonian terminology, which are provided in this book.

The terminology section does not include all the words, characters and symbols used in reading the Bakht. What you will find in the terminology section of this book, is the list and explanation of the meaning of key-words used exclusively in this volume.

27

This revised volume contains additional terminology and definitions of keywords.

You should memorize by heart the meaning of all the Bakht words and expressions, before you practice and/or read Bakht.

Readings are neither complete nor meaningful if you forget the meanings of the Bakht words and expressions, or if you try to guess the meaning.

Guessing or interpreting the meaning of words, symbols, cards and line-up of the Deck Card will confuse you and disorient you.

So you better start reading the section of terminology, before reading any other part of this book.

⌘⌘⌘

2. How many pages should you read at one time?

Because it is a subject totally unknown to you, and because a deep and complete study of the Bakht requires memorization of all the archaic words to be used in reading the Bakht, and the meanings of numerous symbols, letters and characters, you should read only a few pages each time; twenty pages would suffice, assuming that you will read them more than once in a single sitting.

⌘⌘⌘

3. Keep a notebook handy:

You are going to need it, especially for taking notes about meanings of cards and symbols you are not sure about, or you have forgotten. The notebook should also be used for drawing the Tarot cards' symbols. You have to remember all those symbols by heart. The best way to do it is to keep on writing down and drawing the symbols, letters and characters found on each card. You should also write down all the questions that concern you; go back to the book, find the answers, and write them in the notebook. This exercise is extremely useful.

In your notebook, you should constantly work on Tarot cards configurations, line-ups, and layout. I recommend that in your mind, hand-pick two to three cards, draw them on a separate page of the notebook, and read the Bakht. Go back to the book to find out if your reading is accurate. If not, correct your answers, and write them down in the notebook. And as you progress, you are going to find out, that the notebook is an essential learning tool.

⌘⌘⌘

4. More questions and unfound answers.

This revised volume introduces you to the hidden world of Bakht. An immense world of knowledge, wisdom and secret para-normal faculties. However, this first part of the series does not include all the Dirasaat and techniques. Consequently, you might not find the answers to all your questions, especially if you have an inquisitive mind, and you are of a curious nature. Don't get frustrated. Write down your questions in your notebook. You will be able to find the answers, after you have practiced enough on the configurations, layout, and line-up of the cards.

It is impossible to explain in one volume, everything about the Bakht. This first part should be enough for now.

This revised edition will complete your Dirasaat. The second volume will guide you toward more answers and additional explanations, especially when your cards give you mixed messages.

In addition, there is a very useful and informative section in volume two "Q&A" that could answer all your questions.

The "Q&A" section was taken from Ulema Kiraat, and questions/answers from the Ulema Jamiya training sessions.

The novices and students of the Ulema are as inquisitive as you are. They have asked their teachers all sorts of questions. And you are going to benefit from their questions, and the answers of the enlightened masters.

⌘ ⌘ ⌘

5. Cutting out the cards pages from this book.

You will be asked to cut out several pages from volume 2 (Part 2). These pages are those which contain your Tarot Cards. You must cut out all these pages, and laminate each card, one by one. Of course, you could always xerox these pages, but I strongly recommend that you cut out the cards pages to preserve the correct alignment, dimensions and positions of the Tarot cards.

⌘ ⌘ ⌘

6. Where and how to store your cards.

It is extremely important that you protect your cards from the elements, and do not allow others to touch your Tarot Card Deck. The cards should only absorb your own vibes.

Other people's vibes will contaminate the deck.

Wrap your cards in a piece of silk, and place the piece of silk in a wooden box. At the very beginning, keep the box under your pillow for 24 hours.

Do the same things after having received your laminated cards back from the lamination shop.

During the reading session, and especially at the very beginning of the reading, the other person who is asking you to read his/her Bakht must touch the deck of the card. This should be done only once, at the very beginning of the séance. If the received answers are not satisfactory, ask the Taleb to touch the deck of the cards one more time.

You, the Kareh, make sure that the Taleb touches the cards after he/she has already asked his/her question.

⌘ ⌘ ⌘

⌘ Terminology ⌘

Getting acquainted with Bakht and Ana'kh terminology.

Learning the terminology of the Ulema Anunnaki Tarot is a must. In the process of explaining how it works, we will be using Anakh words.

Thus, getting yourself acquainted with the Bakht and Ana'kh terminology before reading the next chapters and/or any lesson in this book is a must!

⌘ ⌘ ⌘

⌘ Terminology ⌘

Getting acquainted with Bakht and Ana'kh terminology.

- ❖ **Afrit:** Entities created by the Anunnaki. Some Afrit resemble the Djins.

- ❖ **Ana'kh:** Language of the Anunnaki.

- ❖ **Arwah:** Spirits and non-human entities.

- ❖ **Baal-Shamroutim:** The teachers of the Ba-khaat or Bakhaati, also called Tahiriim.

- ❖ **Ba-khaat or Bakhaati:** The 700 remaining persons who practice the Bakht.

- ❖ **Bakht Haya.Ti:** Linear future.

- ❖ **Bakht:** Foreseeing, foretelling or reading the future by using Ulema techniques.

- ❖ **Difaya:** Protection shield, created by your active Conduit (for your own protection, physically and mentally.)

- ❖ **Dirasaat**: Studies.

- ❖ **Fath:** Opening up the pockets of Zaman "Time".

- ❖ **Hader:** The present.

- ❖ **Idkhal:** Opening up the pockets of Zaman "Time".

- ❖ **Ikbal:** The future.

- ❖ **Ilmu Al Donia**: Science or Knowledge of the Universe.

- ❖ **Istimrar**: Time continuum (Space-Time).

- ❖ **Jamiya:** An Ulema society.

- ❖ **Kareh:** The reader of the Bakht.

- ❖ **Khilek, 'Ilek:** Born, trapped.

- ❖ **Kiraat:** Readings, lectures.

- ❖ **Kitbu:** What it is written for your future.

- ❖ **Ma'had:** Ulema center of learning.

- ❖ **Madi:** The past.

- ❖ **Maktoob, Al:** What is was written in your future.

- ❖ **Mirach:** The past.

- ❖ **Mounawariin:** The enlightened Ulema; one of the 4 categories of the Ulema Anunnaki.

- ❖ **Mourabaiyaat:** The four squares of the Tarot Table.

- ❖ **Moustakbal Daaem:** Multidimensional future.

- ❖ **Moustakbal:** The future.

- ❖ **Nimar**: The Ulema Anunnaki Numerology Chart.

- ❖ **Ramiyaat:** The act of throwing. More precisely the throwing of one Bakht card on the Tarot Table.

- ❖ **Ramiyah:** The line-up of the cards.

- ❖ **Rouhaniyiin**: A title for the medieval and some contemporary alchemists/Kabalists.

- ❖ **Sadika:** The truth, or the correct answer.

- ❖ **Sharif:** The noble in spirit and thoughts.

- ❖ **Sifra:** Segment of your life.

- ❖ **Sifra Ardi or Erdu:** Segment of your life on Earth.

- ❖ **Sifra Donia:** Segment of your life from the moment it was fashioned by the Anunnaki.

- ❖ **Sifra Falaki:** Segment of your life outside the physical world.

- ❖ **Sinhar:** An Anunnaki lord.

- ❖ **Sinhar Khaldi:** Early Chaldean priests/astrologers/astronomers.

- ❖ **Soura**: Cosmic copies of a living entity, human or other life-forms in other or multiple dimensions.

- ❖ **Ta-Adul:** Equilibrium.

- ❖ **Tahar:** Early Phoenician Purification priests.

- ❖ **Tahiriim:** The teachers of the Ba-khaat or Bakhaati, also called the "Pure Masters, or the Purified Masters".

- ❖ **Takaarub:** Chronological time-rhythm of the Ulema Anunnaki.

- ❖ **Takasur:** Multidimensional occurrences.

- ❖ **Taleb:** The person who is asking you to read his/her Bakht.

- ❖ **Warakat Al Haz:** The 10 Cards of Good Fortune.

- ❖ **Woujoud:** Existence.

- ❖ **Zaman:** Time.

- ❖ **Zaman Istimraar**: Time-space continuum; the past, present and future are timelines that exist and run concurrently.

- ❖ **Zikra:** Memory.

⌘⌘⌘

On the concept of Fikr and the Double

Fik'r is the ability of reading future events and others' thoughts
Derived from the Anakh Fik-R'r, and Fik.Ra.Sa. The esoteric Arabic word "Firasa" is derived from Fik.Ra.Sa. It means in Arabic the ability to read thoughts, to understand the psyche of a person just by looking at him/her. The Ulema uses Fik'r to read the mind, to learn about the intentions of others, and assess the level of intelligence of people.

As defined in the "Anunnaki Encyclopedia" (Authored by M. de Lafayette), and according to the doctrine and Kira'at of the Ulema, the soul is an invention of early humans who needed to believe in a next life. It was through the soul that mortals could and would hope to continue to live after death.

Soul as an element or a substance does not exist anywhere inside the human body. Instead, there is a non-physical substance called "Fik'r" that makes the brain function, and it is the brain that keeps the body working, not the soul. The "Fik'r" was the primordial element used by the Anunnaki at the time they created the final form of the human race.

Fik'r was not used in the early seven prototypes of the creation of mankind according to the Sumerian texts. Although The "Fik'r", is the primordial source of life for our physical body, it is not to be considered as DNA, because DNA is a part of "Fik'r"; DNA is the physical description of our genes, a sort of a series of formulas, numbers and sequences of what there in our body, the data and history of our genes, genetic origin, ethnicity, race, so on. Thus Fik'r includes DNA.

Ulema said: "Consider Fik'r as a cosmic-sub-atomic-intellectual-extraterrestrial (Meaning non-physical, non-earthly) depot of all what it constituted, constitutes and shall continue to constitute everything about you.

And it is infinitesimally small. However, it can expand to an imaginable dimension, size and proportions. It stays alive and continues to grow after we pass away if it is still linked to the origin of its creation, in our case the Anunnaki.

The Fik'r is linked to the Anunnaki our creators through a "Conduit" found in the cells of the brain. For now, consider Fik'r as a small molecule, a bubble. After death, this bubble leaves the body. In fact, the body dies as soon as the bubble leaves the body. The body dies because the bubble leaves the body. Immediately, with one tenth of one million of a second, the molecule or the bubble frees itself from any and everything physical, including the atmosphere, the air, and the light; absolutely everything we can measure, and everything related to earth, including its orbit.

39

The molecule does not go before St. Paul, St. Peter or God to stand judgment and await the decision of God -whether you have to go to heaven or hell– because there is no hell and there is no heaven the way we understand hell and heaven. So it does not matter whether you are a Muslim, a Christian, a Jew, a Buddhist or a believer in any other religion. The molecule (Bubble) enters the original blueprint of "YOU"; meaning the first copy, the first sketch, the first formula that created you. Humans came from a blueprint. Every human being has a Double.

Your double is a copy stored in the "Rouh-Plasma"; an enormous compartment under the control of the Anunnaki on Ashtari and can be transported to another star, if Ashtari ceases to exist. And this double is immortal. In this context, human is immortal, because its Double never dies. Once the molecule re-enters your original copy (Which is the original You), you come back to life with all your faculties, including your memory, but without physical, emotional and sensorial properties (The properties you had on earth), because they are not perfect."

Ulema Sadiq said: "At that time, and only at that time, you will decide whether you want to stay in your Double or go somewhere else...the universe is yours. If your past life on earth accumulated enough good deeds such as charity, generosity, compassion, forgiveness, goodness, mercy, love for animals, respect for nature, gratitude, fairness, honesty, loyalty...then your Double will have all the wonderful opportunities and reasons to decide and select what shape, format, condition you will be in, and where you will continue to live." In other words, you will have everything, absolutely everything and you can have any shape you want including a brand new corporal form. You will be able to visit the whole universe and live for ever, as a mind, as an indestructible presence, and also as a non-physical, non- earthly body, but you can still re-manifest yourself in any physical body you wish to choose.

Worth mentioning here, that the molecule, (So-called soul in terrestrial term) enters a new dimension by shooting itself into space and passing through the "Baab", a sort of a celestial star-gate or entrance.

If misguided, your molecule (So-called your soul) will be lost for ever in the infinity of time and space and what there is between, until reconnected to your prototype via the "Miraya".

⌘ ⌘ ⌘

⌘ What is Bakht? ⌘

Bakht: Reading the Future
⌘

❖ **Your future already exists in another dimension.**
❖ **Knowing the past is essential for reading the future.**
❖ **Linear Future and Multidimensional Future.**

41

⌘ What is Bakht? ⌘

Bakht: Reading the Future
⌘

Your future already exists in another dimension.

Bakht is the Ana'kh word of reading and/or foretelling a Sifra "Segment of your life", in the present or in the future. Although, only the ultimate enlightened masters (Mounawariin) can accomplish this task, many of us can in some instances learn about future events to occur in our lives, if we follow the instructions of the Mounawariin in, and/or outside the Ma'had (Ulema Center of Learning).

The Ashraaf (Plural of Sharif) "The noble in spirit and thoughts" would also have the ability to glance at the future, if the Bakht Dirasaat (Studies of the texts) are consulted, even though Ulema's instructions were not directly provided. But their access to the future would be limited, but not minimal.

This book should help you in your journey.

The future is neither concealed, nor hidden, because the future has already happened in a zone or Zamania that exists very close to the zone or sphere of existence, that you already live in. In other words, the past, present and future are timelines that exist and run concurrently, called Istimraar.

⌘ ⌘ ⌘

43

Knowing the past is essential for reading the future.

Foreseeing, foretelling and/or reading the future implies full knowledge of past events in your life. You might wonder why knowing the past is essential for reading the future.

It is important because you, as a human being have never left the past. For example, a pleasant or unpleasant experience that happened to you in this world in 1981, in New York City, will reoccur in a different space-time zone, located in a different world that either already coexists with this physical world you live in, has existed in 1848 (Or another year), or will exist in five thousand years from now.

Does this mean that every event is constantly being repeated indefinitely in different worlds, dimensions and times? Yes, it is, according to mainstream science and quantum physics – based upon the theory of the "Ever expanding universe." –

And according to the Ulema Anunnaki, people (Humans and other life-forms) live simultaneously on different Woujoud and Zaman. Most certainly, they might look different, physically and bio-organically, because of the atmospheric and climate conditions, and they could or would act differently –convergent or divergent– according to the level of their awareness and intelligence in different worlds.

Consequently, you can live a past on this Earth and remember very well past events in your life, and in the same time, you remain unaware of your other existences, other pasts and lives in different worlds.

Henceforth, you must learn what has happened or what is currently happening to you, or to your other copies, either on different planets and habitats, or in higher dimensions.

Now, you begin to know that each one of us has infinite copies of ourselves, as well as, many separate and independent past(s).

The Ulema Anunnaki Bakht will help you retrace and find your multiple existences, including, your past, your present and your future. In this sense, the Bakht is different from all other divination methods and Tarots known to man.

⌘ ⌘ ⌘

Linear Future and Multidimensional Future.

Knowing the future and revisiting your past in different dimensions and previous lives is a pre-requisite for reading your Bakht Haya.Ti (Linear Future), and Moustakbal Daa-em (Multidimensional Future).

There are some events in your past that greatly influence the course of your life, and part of your future. The situation gets a little bit tricky, when you are not fully aware of major events, and decisions you have made in your Moustakbal Daa-em, because few of us are capable of visiting our past(s) in different dimensions.

The future in its two forms, linear and multidimensional is what really constitutes your true future. However, it is not absolutely necessary to learn about all the phases of your past, and what your Double or your other copies in different time-space zones have done in the past, and/or are currently doing in a zone beyond Earth.

If you believe that life continues after death, then it becomes necessary to learn about your Double, and other bio-organic and etheric copies of yourself that currently exist in other worlds.

⌘ ⌘ ⌘

Reading our Future and our Freedom on Earth

⌘ ⌘

❖ Do we have one future or multiple futures?
❖ Are we trapped in this life?
❖ Are we the slaves of a Supreme Creator?
❖ Can we change our future and create our own destiny, without upsetting God?
❖ Can Bakht reading help us free ourselves and learn about our future?

Bakht, reading our future and our freedom on Earth.

> ❖ Do we have one future or multiple futures?
> ❖ Are we trapped in this life?
> ❖ Are we the slaves of a Supreme Creator?
> ❖ Can we change our future and create our own destiny, without upsetting God?
> ❖ Can Bakht reading help us free ourselves and learn about our future?

⌘ ⌘ ⌘

On Earth, in this world, we have one single future. The learned Ulema referred to it as Al Maktoob, meaning what was written. This concept has created an intellectual, philosophical and religious controversy, even an outrage, for all those who have rejected the idea that a Supreme Creator has already imposed upon us, a future, the moment we were born; a future that controls our destiny and our life, for ever!

In other words, what it is already written in the front-page of our life, dictates the magnitude, level and development of our future successes, failures, kind of job or profession reserved for us, our health conditions, finances, families, how good or how bad our children will be in the future, sort and amount of joy and pain we will feel in the forthcoming years of our lives, so on…

Others have felt that the Al Maktoob makes us slaves of the Creator, because our destiny has been decided upon, without our knowledge, consent and will.

If this is the case, then our life has no purpose at all, and no matter how hard we try to reach a higher level of spirituality and awareness, we will always fail because, it was written in the book of our future, that we have no choice, no freedom to choose and above all, it was already written, that our efforts in this context were not to bear fruit. Thus, it becomes impossible for any of us to change our future, and/or re-write what it is already written and decided upon, in the book of life and destiny.

Consequently, learning about our Bakht (Future) would not serve any purpose, except to make us feel trapped in this life. This is what many people, and some of the early Gnostics have felt about this unpleasant and horrible scenario. But the Ulema Anunnaki have a different scenario for all of us; a pleasant and a happy one.

Humans have retained their freedom of choice, thus, they are accountable for all their actions, deeds, intentions and thoughts. They have the right and the freedom to choose, select and carry on their own plans. And in the process of doing so, they remain the masters of their own destiny, and solely responsible for their decisions, and the consequences of these decisions.

Their mental faculties and degree of their creativity are shaped by, and decided upon by many factors, such as the Conduit, the Jabas, and the Fikr. But their destiny and future remain unconditioned by the DNA, the Conduit and other genetic "ingredients" fashioned by the Anunnaki.

The ethical-moral-spiritual endeavors and aspects of their physical and non-physical structures remain under their personal control. This part of their future can be learned about and read by using the Bakht.

In addition, humans' present and future decisions and actions, and the consequences of their deeds and intentions could be altered or changed, according to their free will and personal choices.

All these decisions, deeds, intentions, consequences, and effects are part of one single future, which can be changed at will. But the remaining part of their future which is conditioned by the genetic formula of the Anunnaki cannot be changed, unless the Conduit is fully activated

Reading the Bakht, guides you in this direction, and explains to you what part of your future can be changed, and what part of your future will remain intact.

This, applies exclusively to your future on Earth; your Erdi future.

So, are we trapped in this life?

Are we at the mercy of the Anunnaki?

Is our life, destiny and future already decided upon, by the Anunnaki who created us by using multiple genetic techniques and experiments?

Do we have the power, the choice and the freedom to change our future? If so, is it the whole future or part of it?

You will find the answers to these questions while you are reading your Bakht. And step by step, you will learn what is going to happen to you in this life, in the present, in the near future, and in the distant future, simply because your present and future exist simultaneously as you read your Bakht.

In addition, when you consult the Ulema Anunnaki Tarot on different subjects and matters of concern, the cards will tell you what you should do and consider, and what you should avoid. It will become crystal clear, and future events will be displayed right before your eyes.

You have to remember that the Ulema Anunnaki Tarot is a reading of many of your futures; one on Earth, and the others in different zones of times and spaces.

I think, for now, you should be concerned only with your Erdi future, which is here on Earth, where you live.

51

As you progress in this field of Ulema Tarot, and as you begin to learn more about other dimensions, and copies of yourself in other worlds, your mind will start to understand gradually how things work in different dimensions, and particularly how you and part of your multidimensional futures are projected.

⌘ ⌘ ⌘

⌘ Your Name ⌘

Your Name Here and Beyond
⌘

- ❖ **Ismu Ardi; your name on Earth.**
- ❖ **Ismu Khalka; your non-Earth name.**
- ❖ **Searching for your name in Ana'kh.**

⌘ Your Name ⌘
Your Name Here and Beyond
⌘

In this chapter, I will talk to you about:

> ❖ Ismu Ardi; your name on Earth.
> ❖ Ismu Khalka; your non-Earth name.
> ❖ The importance of your given name.
> ❖ The importance of a name you have received from a higher source, before you were born, and which you are not aware of.

⌘ ⌘ ⌘

Ismu Ardi; your name on Earth.

Your current name is not necessarily your true name, because it was a name chosen and given to you by your parents or relatives.

In many parts of the globe, and especially in the Middle East, a name is usually given to a new born to honor the name and memory of a father or the head of a family.

In tribal and rigidly traditional communities, a person is often referred to, and/or called as "Ben" of (in Judaic-Jewish tradition) or "Bin" of, and "Ibn" of (in Arabic and Muslim tradition), meaning the son of.

Thus, a name could be given for traditional and familial reasons. We call this, Ismu Ardi, meaning a terrestrial name.

The Ismu Ardi is not your primordial or original name.

⌘ ⌘ ⌘

Ismu Khalka; your non-Earth name.
Searching for your name in Ana'kh.

> Regardless of your ethnicity, your native tongue, gender or race, you have a name that is written in Ana'kh, which is the Anunnaki's language. This name is a code; your DNA code.
>
> In many of the Semitic and ancient Middle Eastern languages, one's name is usually an adjective; an attribute, rather than a noun. For instance, the name Kabir means big; the name Asad means lion, and so on.

In Ana'kh, names given to people are an attribute, a sort of code. In other words, the name refers to attributes and faculties found in your DNA, and stored in the Conduit of your brain, as it was explained to us by the Ulema Anunnaki. This name is called "Ismu Khalka"; your non-Earth name, assigned to you by the Anunnaki.

Each one of us has a name, that nobody else has.
There are many Roberts and many Janes on Earth, but in the Anunnaki's realm and in the Bakht (Tarot), there is only one Jane, and only one Robert.
Meaning, if your assigned name is Muktiar, nobody else is called Muktiar. You are the only person in other dimensions who has the Muktiar name.
Why?

Because Muktiar or other names assigned to other people are in fact a code, some sort of mathematical-genetic formula.

And each person in the Donia (Life, universe, multiverse, etc.) has a different genetic formula and DNA, just like your fingerprints. Thus, for each genetic formula, and for each person's DNA, there is only one name (Code).

On Earth, your name could be Albert or Khalid, Lydia or Hind, but in another dimension, or in a different world, you have a different name totally unrelated to the name you have on Earth.

You are Albert on Earth, but you are also Shimradu in the next dimension, Rafaat in a parallel dimension, and Kira in a non-bio-organic form of existence. Three different names for the same person, so on.

Are Albert, Shimradu and Rafaat the same person?

Yes and no.

Yes, because all of the three have retained some similar and major properties and characteristics, such as the Conduit, the Fikr, the Jabas, etc.

No, because all of the three now have different properties, such as new cellular memory, new molecules, totally different organic substance, more organs, less organs, etc.

⌘ ⌘ ⌘

The changes occur at so many different levels.

For instance, on Earth, you have two eyes, while in a different world, eyes are no longer needed to see objects; they have been replaced by other organs or tissues totally inconceivable and incomprehensible to the human mind.

And because the new Albert has become a new entity, the future of this new entity becomes diametrically different from the future of a person called Albert who once upon a time lived on Earth, or is still living somewhere on Earth.

Consequently, for each new entity, new person, or a new intelligent life form, a new Bakht has been created. But do not be concerned with this for now. All what you have to do for the moment is to find the name, the Anunnaki gave you when you were first born or conceived.

This very name is the one I recommend to use while reading your Bakht and Tarot charts.

Yet, you can still use your Erdi name to read your Bakht and learn a lot about your future. But you have to remember that by only using your Ismu Erdi, your access to the complete file of your future and destiny will not be complete. Nevertheless, what you would or could discover about yourself and your future is mind-boggling.

⌘ ⌘ ⌘

⌘How do I write my name in Anakh?⌘
⌘

❖ **How can I find my true name (Code); the one the Anunnaki gave me before I was born?**

59

⌘ How do I write my name in Anakh? ⌘ ⌘

It is not easy, but it is possible.

❖ First, you must equate the letters of your name with the corresponding letters in Anakh/Proto-Ugaritic. Look at the corresponding alphabet chart on page 63.

❖ Second, place the letters of your name under each corresponding letter in the Anakh/Proto-Ugaritic; several examples are provided in this book.

❖ Third: Write your Anakh name from right to left, the way the Anakh language is written, similar to written Hebrew and Arabic.

This exercise gives you your name in Anakh, and refers you to a pertinent meaning. However, it does not give you the primordial name (Code), the Anunnaki assigned to you when you were born, even before you were born/conceived in a blueprint.

⌘ ⌘ ⌘

How could I find my true name (Code); the one the Anunnaki gave me before I was born?

You will find out in volume two of this series.

⌘ ⌘ ⌘

61

Writing/Equating Your Name in Anakh/Proto-Ugaritic
⌘ ⌘ ⌘

Chart of the Latin alphabet versus the Ana'kh letters.

⌘ Writing/Equating Your Name in Anakh/Proto-Ugaritic ⌘

Chart

A	B	C	D	E	F	G	H

I	J	K	L	M	N	O	P

Q	R	S	T	U	V	W	X

Y	Z

Additional Sounds/Letters

H   Ayn   Sh "Shin" Ni

Full explanation of these four additional characters is provided in volume 2. Do not be concerned with this for the moment.

⌘ ⌘ ⌘

⌘ Placing the letters of your name under each corresponding letter in the Anakh/Proto-Ugaritic ⌘

Exercise #1:

Let's assume that you name is Mary, and you are trying to find its equivalent or corresponding name in Anakh/Proto-Ugaritic, the language we will be using for the Tarot.

First: Search for the corresponding letter for M.

The corresponding letter is:

Second: Search for the corresponding letter for A.

The corresponding letter is:

Third: Search for the corresponding letter for R.

The corresponding letter is:

Fourth: Search for the corresponding letter for Y.

The corresponding letter is:

67

Exercise #2:

First: Write now your Anakh name from right to left. You should get this:

Second: Find the numerical value for each letter.

ⵎ   =**M**

M: The numerical value for the letter M is 13.
Meaning:
1-Your physical strength is bigger than your mental strength. But if you are patient, and you try again with determination and a deep concentration, you will gain more mental power.
2-Tenderness and affection.

ⴾ =**A**

A: The numerical value for the letter A is 1.
Meaning:
1-The beginning.
2-It is a good time to start a business.
3-Change of status quo.

ⵊ =**R**

R: The numerical value for the letter R is 18.
Meaning:
1-You are a candidate to play a major role in your field, and leave a huge mark in this area.
2-You are going to face strong opposition in your most important projects. Such opposition will come from the opposite sex. And it will occur on the job, or where you work, such as an office, an organization, and even during a delegation and a public speech. But you will be able to convince others and eliminate that opposition if this happens on these days: Tuesday, Thursday and Friday.
3-Monday is not a lucky day for you.

 =Y

Y: The numerical value for the letter Y is 10 .
Meaning:
1-Avoid major decisions on a Monday.
2-Tuesday, Thursday and Friday are your lucky days.
3-Your meticulous planning blends perfectly with an exquisite taste and an accentuated fantasy, yet not totally irrational.
On the contrary, it adds originality and creates a special aura around you.
4-In your life, you will meet strong oppositions.
But with determination you will prevail.

⌘ ⌘ ⌘

And what if you write your name like this: Marie, Myriam or Maria, instead of Mary?

Does this change affect your situation and Bakht?

Absolutely not.

To be sure, repeat the same exercises, and you will find out. No knowledge, no results and no interpretation should be obtained or caused by coincidence or probability.

Even though these exercises might appear incomprehensible and/or irrational, the time will come when you will find out that there are convincing elements, evidence and logic working behind the Bakht techniques.

⌘ ⌘ ⌘

⌘ The Best Time to Read Your Future ⌘
Days and Hours
⌘

❖ You can't use the Bakht Tarot cards all the time.
❖ On Earth, you are simply a copy of yourself.
❖ Recommended days and hours for reading your Bakht.

⌘ The Best Time to Read Your Future ⌘
Days and Hours

You can't use the Bakht Tarot cards all the time.

You can't use the Bakht Tarot cards all the time. It is neither a game nor an amusement. If you do not follow this rule, you will become subject to delusion and illusion.

There are specific days and hours, when and where your future could and would be revealed to you. And once again, let me remind you that knowing your real name and placing it on the "Master Card" is a pre-requisite, if you want to unlock many secrets about your lives, and/or multiple existences in different time-space zones. You must use your "Primordial Name", not your Erdi name.

This is very essential if you want to know what is going to happen to you, here on Earth, or in other dimension(s).

This could seem unrealistic and even bizarre, but consider the possibility that you, as an existing entity on Earth, are linked to another entity which is primordially the true personality/persona of what and who you are.

On Earth, you are simply a copy of yourself.

On Earth, you are simply a copy of yourself, and many of the things you see here on Earth are illusion.

Your "Primordial Entity" has a name and very particular properties. This entity must be brought to the Bakht cards. And you can do it very easily, if you use it/his/her original name. However, using your Earth's name would suffice in most cases.

Recommended days and hours for reading your Bakht.

You have to follow the Takaarub "Chronological time-rhythm of the Ulema Anunnaki" to find the recommended days and hours for reading your Bakht and consulting the Tarot.
Reading the Bakht is not entertainment. It is a serious matter. There are lots of metaphysical and esoteric elements, secrets, and "things" that are closely associated with reading the Tarot.

The Tarot will not "open up", unless you respect and follow the rule of Fath or Idkhal, which means opening up the pockets of Zaman (Time).

Everything around you, even light and shadow are made out of time pockets. Your memories too are made out of time pockets. So, if you want to learn about your future, you must first understand how time enters and exits those pockets, because you are part of it.

In the West, you have sayings that go like this "Time is not on his side", "Wrong place, wrong time", or "There is a time for everything." And there is a deep truth in these sayings. You have to work with time and its vibrations, if you want to find your place in time and space.
The Ulema Anunnaki Tarot will lead you toward your place in time and space. But to accomplish this, you have to find the perfect time to enter your "Own time-space zone."
And this could be done if you align yourself with two things:
1-The Jabas

2-The serenity of the moment, which means, finding a quiet place, where your thoughts are not interrupted or disturbed by others.

Volume two of this series provides techniques and training to accomplish this, as well as a chart to consult, in order to find the most suitable days and hours to open up the reading of your Bakht.

⌘ ⌘ ⌘

⌘ The Tarot Deck⌘
Characteristics
⌘

❖ Generalities.
❖ Bakht and its relation to the inner bio-rhthym and the Anunnaki.

⌘ The Tarot Deck⌘
Characteristics
⌘

Generalities:

❖ Card deck: 25 cards, consisting of a duplicate full deck. Meaning, you must copy the Tarot deck twice to get 50 cards. In other words, you must have two identical cards for each letter or symbol.

❖ All the cards have symbols, numbers, and illustrations indicating one or more meanings, which are explained in this book.

❖ The cards that have a number will be used, in case you get a negative reading, predicting a dangerous event to happen in the present and/or near future, and/or requiring additional opportunities to reverse a bad reading, or altering a forthcoming event.

❖ The "Master Card": It is a blank card reserved for your photo or the photo of a person you wish to learn about, and/or discover his/her intentions, preferences, priorities and persona.

⌘ ⌘ ⌘

Use it discreetly, and always with good intentions. And bear in mind that you cannot alter or affect his/her present or future, but can simply acquire vital information about his/her character and related matters.

❖ The Anunnaki-Ulema have used a very unique "Divination" method to explore ultra-dimension.

❖ The word divination is not totally correct, but we are going to use it for now, because it is "As close as it gets to the real thing," said Ulema Bukhtiar. We can also use the word "Oracle", if you want; basically all these words refer to the same thing in essence.

❖ The term "Ultra-dimension" means a "Surrounding that is not normally and usually detected by scientific or physical means," said Ulema Seif El Din.

❖ This ultra-dimension belongs to the realm of many things, including thoughts, perception, extra-sensitive feelings (Not caused by anomaly of any sort), and a depot of knowledge that evolves around past, present and future events.

❖ One of the aspects of the Ulema's Kira'at that deals with Tarot reading is called Bak'ht-Kira'at. The Master taps into a zone that contains lots of information about events to occur in the future. The figures and numbers he/she opens up while reading the cards are closely related to that zone called "Da-irat Al-Maaref" (Circumference of Knowledge).

❖ The figures and numbers that appear on the card guide the Master reader toward a chart that contains and explains all the possible meanings, NOT interpretation.

❖ "But this is not enough, we should not rely only on symbols and numbers, because this could happen in a very ordinary manner, far from the truthful reach of knowledge and discovery…it could fall into the possibility of coincidences. This is why, a reading should be repeated multiple times to detect coincidence and separate superstitions from reality..." explained the Honorable Ulema Ghandar.

❖ The Ulema cards are personalized, meaning they are hand-made by you. You do not purchase your Ulema cards from stores. They are not a commercial product. The Master provides you with a set of 25 cards, called "Warka".

❖ Each card has either a figure or a symbol (Number). The cards are printed on a master-sheet or on several sheets. You must cut each card individually, until you have 25 cards. You will find the cards (Tarot Deck) in volume 2.

❖ This constitutes your personal card deck. Nobody else should touch or use this deck. The Master will instruct you to attach one of your photos to one specific card. You can place your photo on that card and xerox it, and later add it to the deck. This card is extremely important, because the whole deck will rotate around it.

❖ Something else: One of the 25 cards must bear your name. Also, you should give yourself a new surname. Nobody should know about your new name; it should remain secret.

⌘⌘⌘

What we have so far is this:
❖ a-A set of 25 cards, cut and laminated by you.
❖ b-One of the cards which has your photo.
❖ c-One of the cards which has your real name (First name).
❖ d-One of the cards which has your new name. (The one you gave yourself)
Now you start to understand why the Ulema cards are called "Personalized".
❖ Would you be able to learn about your future if you use the Ulema Tarot cards?

81

❖ Enough, not everything. First, you have to remember that if your "Conduit" is not activated, your access to knowledge about your future will be very limited.

❖ However, you will be able to learn a lot about some events that are extremely important in your life, and especially about "New happenings or things to happen" that can influence or alter your luck, success, and other vital matters.

❖ The cards will give you some guidance and orientation. The cards will give you dates and a warning related to each separate event to occur in the future; event(s) detected by your cards.

❖ Important note: If you attach the photo of another person to one of the cards, you could possibly discover lots of things about that person. However, you will not able to influence his/her mind, or bring a major change to his/her life, unless some criteria are met.

⌘ ⌘ ⌘

Bakht and its relation to the inner bio-rhthym and the Anunnaki:

Thousands of years ago, before history was recorded, the Anunnaki created the first Man to meet their needs. They created us as a work-force to take care of the fields, cultivate the land, and bring them food; this is according to the Akkadian/Sumerian clay tablets. It is very clear.

At that time, when the Anunnaki gods and goddesses (Aruru, Mummu, Ea, Ninna, etc.) created the first prototypes of the quasi-human races, Man did not have all the mental faculties we have today.

Thus, no Bakht was written for us.

We had no future. And the purpose of our life on Earth was dictated by the Anunnaki. It was not a bright future, and it was limited and fashioned by the intentions of the Anunnaki.

Later on, 13 new faculties were added to the brain of the early Man. And everything in the brain was wired and functioned according to a cellular rhythm.

We cannot change this rhythm.

But we can improve on it, and ameliorate its functioning, by acquiring new knowledge, developing a stronger memory, reading, writing, listening to intelligent and well-informed people, getting rid of bad habits, and elevating our being to a higher mental/spiritual level, through introspection, meditation, and refraining from hurting others.

By doing so, we can free ourselves and reach a higher dimension of knowledge and awareness.

Some people are born normal, others are born with some mental deficiency, while a few were created as geniuses, like Bach, Mozart, etc., people who astonished us with extraordinary creativity, and unmatched talents.

These talents and mental gifts were already "placed" into their Conduit. Otherwise, how can we explain the astonishing musical compositions of Mozart and other great composers at the age of 4?

Yes, we can alter the inner bio-rhthym, the Anunnaki installed in us, but we cannot change it completely. And by altering the rhythm, we can alter part of our future. This can be detected by reading the Bakht.

First thing to do is to activate the Conduit. As far as luck (Good and bad) is concerned, the noble in spirit (Mind, or "Soul" if you want) will be given the opportunities and means to learn how to positively reshape future events in his/her life.

Unfortunately, there are too many good people in the world who are constantly suffering. And we wonder where is the logic? What is the reason for their suffering? Is it true that good people always finish last? Sadly enough, it happens all the time. We see hard-working nurses (Who save lives) struggling to make a living.

We see devoted school teachers unable to pay their bills.We see bloody bastards getting richer and richer, while honorable, loving and caring people are being kicked out of their homes!!

Where is the justice?

The truth I tell you, there is no absolute justice on Earth, despite all the good intentions of so many of us, and despite so many good court decisions, and decent laws to maintain law and order.

*** *** ***

The Ulema taught us that a good behavior, a high level of morality, an unconditional love, forgiveness and generosity do not guarantee success in life, or secure a good luck.

Ulema Badri said verbatim: "Your character and good manners are the only things you should keep even when you have lost everything in life.

So, start developing your brain, activate your Conduit, talk to your inner-self…and there, you will find the salvation… you will find a way to change your bad luck into good luck. If your Mind is in harmony with your "Jaba", then, and only then, you will be able to change your inner bio-rhythm, and influence your DNA's metamorphosis."

And remember, your DNA is a vital part of your future. You can decipher its sequence by reading your Bakht.

⌘ ⌘ ⌘

Pronunciation of letters and symbols of the Tarot Deck
⌘

- ❖ 1. Alef
- ❖ 2. Bett
- ❖ 3. Geem
- ❖ 4. Daa
- ❖ 5. Heh
- ❖ 6. Waw
- ❖ 7. Zaay'n
- ❖ 8. Hahh
- ❖ 9. Theh
- ❖ 10. Yo-Dah
- ❖ 11. Kaa'f
- ❖ 12. Lam
- ❖ 13. Miim
- ❖ 14. Noon
- ❖ 15. Sa-Mekh
- ❖ 16. Eye'n
- ❖ 17. Kop'fh
- ❖ 18. Reshh
- ❖ 19. S'hiin
- ❖ 20. Nee-Ha-Yah
- ❖ 21. Eh
- ❖ 22. Yu
- ❖ 23. Ee
- ❖ 24. Ow
- ❖ 25. Pef

Pronunciation of letters and symbols of the Tarot Deck
⌘

Symbol, Character,
Letter

1. Name: Alef.
Pronunciation: Aleff.

2. Name: Bet "Beth".
Pronunciation: Bett.

3. Name: Gim "Gimel".
Pronunciation: Geem.

4. Name: Daleth "Da".
Pronunciation: Daa

5. Name: He "H".
Pronunciation: Heh.

6. Name: W "Wah".
Pronunciation: Waw.

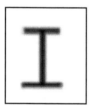

7. Name: Z "Zayn".
Pronunciation: Zaay'n.

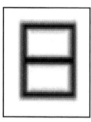

8. Name: H "Hah".
Pronunciation: Hahh or Heh.

9. Name: T "Teh".
Pronunciation: Theh or Teth.

10. Name: Y "Yoda".
Pronunciation: Yo-Dah.

11. Name: K "Kaf"
Pronunciation: Kaa'f.

12. Name: L "Lam".
Pronunciation: Lam and Lamda.

13. Name: M "Mim".
Pronunciation: Mem or Miim.

14. Name: N "Nun".
Pronunciation: Noon.

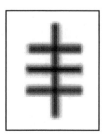

15. Name: S "Samekh".
Pronunciation: Sa-Mekh.

16. Name: Ay'n.
Pronunciation: Eye'n.

17. Name: Q "Koph".
Pronunciation: Kop'fh.

18. Name: R "Resh".
Pronunciation: Reshh.

19. Name: Sh "Shin".
Pronunciation: S'hiin.

20. Name: Ni "Nihaya".
Pronunciation: Nee-Ha-Yah.

21. Name: E "Eh".
Pronunciation: Eh

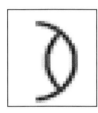

22. Name: U "Uu".
Pronunciation: Yu

23. Name: I "Ii".
Pronunciation: Ee

24. Name: O "O".
Pronunciation: Ow

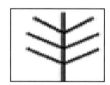

25. Name: P "P".
Pronunciation: Pef, Pt.

⌘ ⌘ ⌘

⌘Ramiyah⌘
The Line-Up of the Cards⌘
⌘⌘⌘

- ❖ The layout of the cards and the line-up of the cards.
- ❖ What is a "Line-up?
- ❖ A warning: Act immediately.

⌘Ramiyah⌘
The Line-Up of the Card⌘
⌘ ⌘ ⌘

1. The layout of the cards and the line-up of the cards.

The layout of the cards on your Tarot Table, is explained step by step in a separate section of this book.

The layout of the cards is not the same as the line-up of the cards on your Tarot Table. You will fully understand what a layout is, and how it works, when you read the section on the layout. So, do not worry about this for now.

⌘ ⌘ ⌘

2. What is a "Line-up?

Line-up is called Ramiyah in Anakh.

Ramiyah means to throw. And Ramiyaat means the act of throwing. More precisely the throwing of the Bakht cards, one after another on the Tarot Table.

A line-up is a combination of two things:

❖ a-The act of placing the cards you have picked up from the Tarot deck (Held in your left hand) in the Mourabaiyaat of the Tarot Table, one after another.
❖ b-The process of reading the four cards placed inside the Mourabaiyaat as a full sentence.

97

A full sentence means: Reading at the same time, your past, your present, your future, and what has been decided upon in the book of your life, in this chronological order. In other words, it is a brief and instant reading of different phases of your Bakht, without an elaborate explanation.

Call it fast reading if you want. But this so-called "fast reading" is extremely important. And I am going to explain to you why it is so important.

You are going to learn later on in this book that, there are several ways, methods and techniques for reading your Bakht, and/or for reading any part, moment, hour, week, year from your life, including your past, present and future.

The "Fast Reading" of the four cards brings together events from the past, the present and the future, and briefly explains to you the reasons for the events and things happening right now, and how things and events could or would change in the future.

It does <u>not</u> tell you what your future is. Nevertheless, the fast reading anchors the reality and the moment you live in.

There are plenty of explanations on the line up in other parts of this books.

⌘ ⌘ ⌘

3. A warning: Act immediately.

> You have placed four cards in the four squares of the Tarot Table. You started to place the cards from right to left. The first square is your PAST, and the last square is WHAT IS DECIDED UPON.

In this fast reading, you have not asked yet any question. And you should not. In other methods of reading, you should ask a question before you lay down any card. But here, you don't.

Now, take a deep breath, relax, and look at all the cards. If you have already memorized by heart the meaning of all the cards, you will be able to understand what each card means. But understanding the meaning of each card separately is not enough in this reading.

You must link or tie together the four different meanings of the four different cards into a sentence.

The sentence you get, is the message or warning, your Tarot is giving you. This is an instant and immediate warning, and you should act or respond accordingly and IMMEDIATELY!

⌘ ⌘ ⌘

Once again, let me repeat this:

This reading is not a reading of your future. It is a message you should take very seriously. The Tarot is telling you what is going on, or what is going to happen in the immediate future. It could be a warning, a good message, a bad message, good news, or bad news. You are the only person who could understand the message. You will not find an explanation of this message if you go back to the book. You should find it in the sentence you have composed from reading the meaning of each card.

You have to work on it. It might not work the first time, but surely it will work perfectly if you keep practicing.

Alexander the Great used this Bakht fast reading, before leading his troops to the battlefield.

Hannibal of Carthage regularly consulted the Tarot fast reading.

The only time he did not, was on the eve of his last battle against the Romans. And you know what happened to him. He was defeated!

Elisha, the Phoenician princess from Tyre, and the founder of the city of Carthage learned about her death from consulting the Bakht fast reading (The cards revealed that she would commit suicide).

Do not be alarmed, do not be frightened, for the Bakht can also bring you good news, a good omen, and give you a rare opportunity to deal with imminent danger, and/or to solve a problem, you thought did not exist.

"No news is good news" is not always correct. Ignoring things, or not receiving necessary information/news could be catastrophic.

⌘ ⌘ ⌘

⌘The Meaning of Each Card⌘
⌘ ⌘ ⌘

❖ Pronunciation.
❖ Corresponding letters in Latin/English.
❖ Numerical value.
❖ Meaning.

⌘Meaning of Each Card⌘

Alef Card, pronounced Aleff.
A in English.
Numerical value: 1.

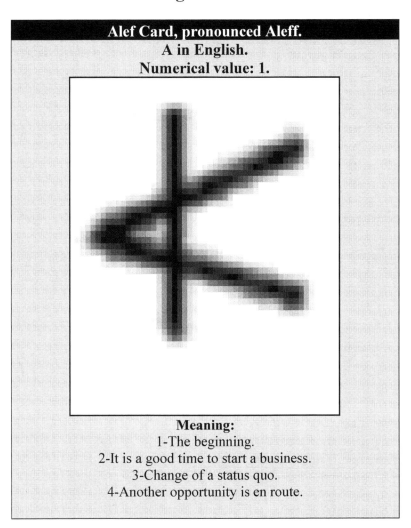

Meaning:
1-The beginning.
2-It is a good time to start a business.
3-Change of a status quo.
4-Another opportunity is en route.

Line up of Alef.

**Reading and explanation of First Line up of Alef
if you get these 4 cards on your Bakht reading table.**

 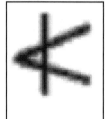  

Meaning:
Total victory, an absolute success.

⌘⌘⌘

Line up of Alef.

Reading and explanation of First Line up of Alef
if you get these 3 cards on your Bakht reading table.

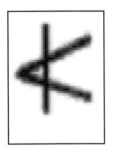 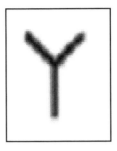 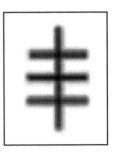

Meaning:
All barriers are removed. You were born very lucky.

⌘ ⌘ ⌘

Line up of Alef.

**Reading and explanation of First Line up of Alef
if you get these 2 cards on your Bakht reading table.**

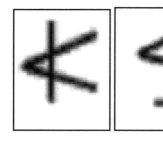

Meaning:
Pursue the project you are working on.
It is going to be very successful.

⌘⌘⌘

Line up of Alef.

Reading and explanation of First Line up of Alef
if you get these 3 cards on your Bakht reading table.

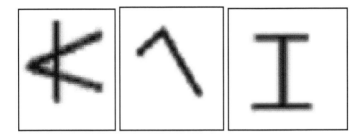

Meaning:
You are strong, and you are going to accomplish magnificent projects. However, because of your arrogance, suspicion and doubts about others, you are going to alienate many friends and allies.

People in this category could lose everything overnight. Because when sudden catastrophes (Especially financial ones) hit them hard, many of their friends and associates will walk away.

The Z Card is clearly telling you: "Time to reconsider what you have done."

⌘⌘⌘

107

Meaning of each card

B "Bet", "Beth" Card, pronounced Bett.
B in English.
Numerical value: 2.

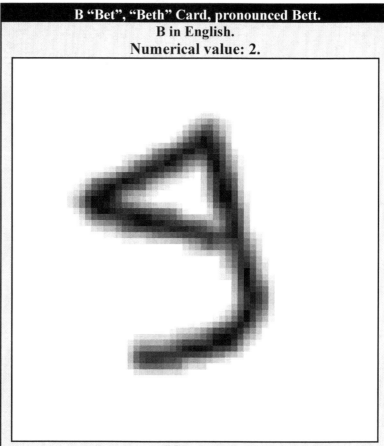

Meaning:

1. Continue/pursue your project.
2. Look at things from a different angle.
3. Consider other or additional possibilities for evaluating an offer you received concerning a new job, or a new location.

Line up of B "Bet", "Beth" Card.

**Reading and explanation of First Line up of Beth
if you get these 3 cards on your Bakht reading table.**

Meaning:
Luck rides with you for the moment. But some strong negative vibes could block your project.
These vibes are emanated from people who are very close to you. And you are partly responsible. The cards are telling you: "Another last chance to change your decision."
Your wish will not be fulfilled if you do not change your strategy.
Those who gave you advice were not well informed. And some of them did not tell you the truth.
You are going to feel lonely and abandoned. It was not a good business relationship.

⌘ ⌘ ⌘

109

Line up of B "Bet", "Beth" Card.

**Reading and explanation of Second Line up of Beth
if you get these 4 cards on your Bakht reading table.**

Meaning:
Luck rides with you for the moment. But avoid major decisions on Monday. It is not a good time for investment, but an excellent moment for planning.
Wait for the forthcoming week to fully understand the situation. Stay quiet for now, but prepare plan b.

⌘ ⌘ ⌘

Meaning of each card

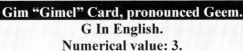

Gim "Gimel" Card, pronounced Geem.
G In English.
Numerical value: 3.

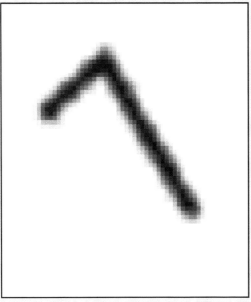

Meaning:
1-Hurting others does not pay. Badmouthing others is an awful deed. The Gim sign is your reminder, because it has witnessed a vicious act you did. So, be prepared to get a taste of your own medicine.

2-You should get rid of the shadows of suspicion and doubts that surround you and disorient your judgment.

3-You are meticulous by nature, however, your indecisiveness could handicap your progress.

Line up of Gim "Gimel" Card.

**Reading and explanation of First Line up of G "Gim"
if you get these 3 cards on your Bakht reading table.**

Meaning:
You did hurt people in the past, and you have caused them
damages and pain. And you are going to pay for it.
Some will come after you.
No way out. Protect yourself.

⌘ ⌘ ⌘

Line up of Gim "Gimel" Card.

**Reading and explanation of Second Line up of G "Gim"
if you get these 3 cards on your Bakht reading table.**

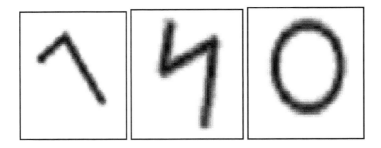

Meaning:
You are still in trouble. And now you are paying your dues. It
happened before, and it is going to happen again.
The current situation is not bright.
Remain determined and strong. For the moment, time is not on
your side, unless you compromise. You will know the outcome
very soon.

⌘ ⌘ ⌘

113

Line up of Gim "Gimel" Card.

**Reading and explanation of Third Line up of G "Gim"
if you get these 3 cards on your Bakht reading table.**

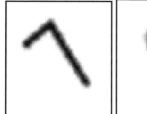  

Meaning:
You are going through a tough time. And you are partially
responsible because of what you have done to others, particularly
close friends and associates.

Get rid of fear and free your mind from negative thoughts. Yes,
you will get some kind of assistance or help, but first, repair the
damages.

Your creativity and/or intelligence creates envy and jealousy
among peers and associates. Always, you should consider more
than one plan of action.

Get your plan a, and your plan b handy, and get rid of arrogance.

⌘ ⌘ ⌘

Meaning of each card

Daleth "Da" Card, pronounced Daa.
D In English.
Numerical value: 4.

Meaning:

1-You have a strong personality. Use it wisely.

2-You are born leader.

3-Logic is not always a security shield. Therefore, unorthodox methods and a new way of thinking could be very beneficial in solving a problem that has lasted for a long time.

4-You are drawn to power. Others too.

Therefore, you should realize that some powerful and jealous people, who are monitoring your success and influence, could hurt you and cripple your success. Watch your enemies once, and your allies twice.

115

Line up of D "Daleth" Card.

Reading and explanation of First Line up of D "Daleth" if you get these 2 cards on your Bakht reading table.

Note: The D is the Anunnaki Delta Symbol/Logo.

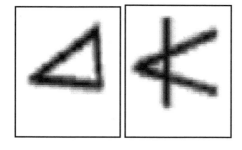

Meaning:
You will dominate the scene.
Outstanding triumph.

⌘ ⌘ ⌘

Line up of Daleth "Da" Card.

Reading and explanation of Second Line up of D "Daleth" if you get these 2 cards on your Bakht reading table.

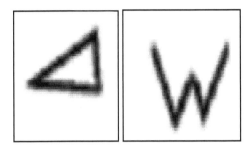

Meaning:
You will be seriously challenged.
Your possibilities are endless.
You will get a good introduction. This will ease up the situation.
Keep your secrets deep in your chest.

⌘⌘⌘

117

Line up of Daleth "Da" Card.

Reading and explanation of Third Line up of D "Daleth" if you get these 3 cards on your Bakht reading table.

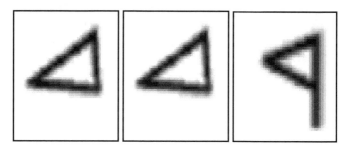

Meaning:
Nobody can stop you now.
You are a candidate to play a major role in your field, and leave a huge mark in this area.
Avoid confrontations on Monday.

⌘⌘⌘

118

Line up of Daleth "Da" Card.

Reading and explanation of the Fourth Line up of D "Daleth", if you get these 2 cards on your Bakht reading table.

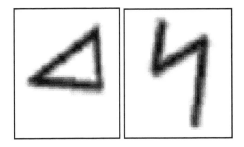

Meaning:
You are leading the way.
You have an opportunity to increase your income, and succeed in new negotiations, but do not meet again with competitors or potential contributors where you have met before.
Change the location.

⌘⌘⌘

119

Meaning of each card

He "H" Card, pronounced Heh.
H in English.
Numerical value: 5.

Meaning:

1-You lack consistency, even though, you are persistent and meticulous.

2-Finish your project before dark.

3-Negative vibes hurt your mental process.

Avoid malicious and argumentative people.

4-Cancel trips if they are scheduled for a late Friday or for an early Saturday.

Line up of He "H" Card.

Reading and explanation of the First Line up of He "H" Card.
If you get these 3 cards on your Bakht reading table.

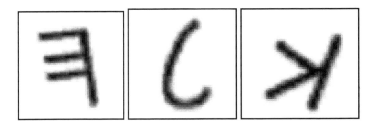

Meaning:
Finish what you have started as soon as possible.
Avoid final decisions on Friday.
A major change will occur by the end of this week, or the next week. Those who in the past, have opposed your views will now side by you.
The situation is not clear for the moment.
Do not rush to conclusions, taking into consideration your limited means. First finish what you have started.

⌘ ⌘ ⌘

121

Line up of He "H" Card.

Reading and explanation of the Second Line up of the He "H" Card.
If you get these 2 cards on your Bakht reading table.

Meaning:
You are behind schedule. It is imperative to complete your project before the end of this week.
You will receive harsh criticism if you do not submit your finished work on Monday.
People who have asked for your support or help are not pleased by the way you have treated them. You have not delivered what you have promised.
Don't turn your friends into bitter and argumentative people. Remember what you have promised them a while ago, and deliver!

⌘⌘⌘

Line up of He "H" Card.

Reading and explanation of the Third Line up of the He "H" Card.
If you get these 3 cards on your Bakht reading table.

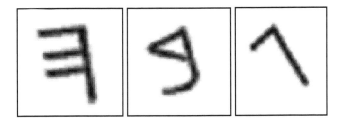

Meaning:
It is safer to stay home this weekend.
Continue or pursue the same project you were working on, and do not consider any other project or plan, before your finish that project.
However, feel free to consider other or additional possibilities for evaluating an offer you have received concerning a new job, or a new location. But you should first finish that project.
You are meticulous by nature, however, your indecisiveness and recent laziness could handicap your progress, and prevent you from getting a promotion, a better pay, or a more challenging position.

⌘⌘⌘

Meaning of each card

W "Wah" Card, pronounced Waw.
W in English.
Numerical value: 6.

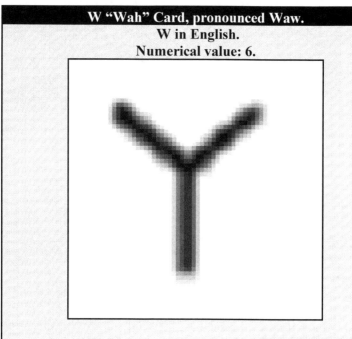

Meaning:

1. The primordial secret symbol of God.
2. Good timing for defending a case, presenting a project, and exploring other possibilities.
3. Peace will be brought to you, and the current difficult moment you are going through will fade away rapidly.
4. Your superior, boss, or a higher authority directly dealing with your business will grant you a big favor.
5. You are idealistic and spiritual. But do not let religious dogma influence your decision.

Reading and explanation of the First Line up of W "Waw".
If you get these 3 cards on your Bakht reading table.

  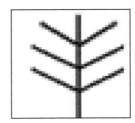

Meaning:
You are idealistic and spiritual. But do not let religious dogma influence your decision.
You will be asked to make a public appearance.
Patience is not one of your major virtues.
Do not rush to conclusions before you refresh your thoughts.
You will meet an unexpected person who is going to change the course of your life. This meeting shall occur in a public place in the early afternoon.
In less than three months from now, you will be asked to make a major decision that could rotate around your home and/or a very unusual relationship. Be prepared, and put all your documents in order.

⌘ ⌘ ⌘

Reading and explanation of the Second Line up of W "Waw".
If you get these 2 cards on your Bakht reading table.

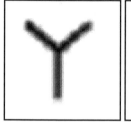 

Meaning:
Although it is a divine sign, two "Waw" could turn your life upside down.
Your good health could deteriorate.
You could loose lots of money.
You could be framed.
However, there is a way to reverse these anticipations: Use the "Adjacent Cards" for additional Bakht reading.

⌘ ⌘ ⌘

Reading and explanation of the Third Line up of W "Waw".
If you get these 2 cards on your Bakht reading table.

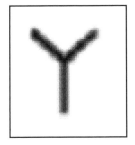 

Meaning:
A sudden change in your life or career.
A change you have feared, and anticipated.
Have you considered plan b?

⌘⌘⌘

Meaning of each card

Z "Zayn", pronounced Zaay'n.
Z in English.
Numerical value: 7

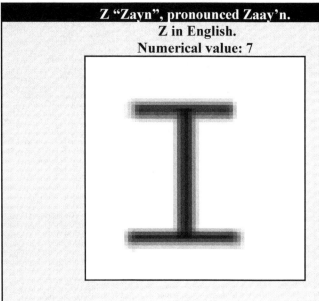

Meaning:

1. The end of a project.
2. The end of a trip.
3. Time to reconsider what you have done.
4. Another last chance to change your decision or statement.

Reading and explanation of the First Line up of Z "Zayn". If you get these 2 cards on your Bakht reading table.

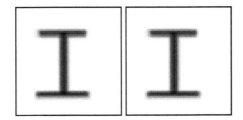

Meaning:
You will be given another chance to redeem yourself.
No reason to fear anything for the moment.
However, others are watching you very closely.
Therefore, you should present a more solid documentation and substantiate your claims without losing your temper.
Do not irritate those who are either investigating you, or asking you to show "good faith."
You will find these documentations in a place you have not searched before.

⌘ ⌘ ⌘

129

**Reading and explanation of the Second Line up of Z "Zayn".
If you get these 3 cards on your Bakht reading table.**

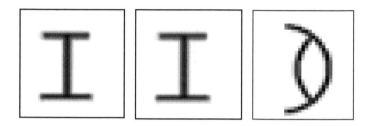

Meaning:
This is your last chance to change your decision or statement.
You have lied in your deposition or you have given a false
statement. And they know about it.
What you have said could hurt you permanently.
There is no way out unless and until you tell the truth.
Seek immediate legal advice.

⌘⌘⌘

**Reading and explanation of the Third Line up of Z "Zayn".
If you get these 3 cards on your Bakht reading table.**

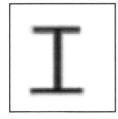 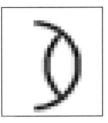 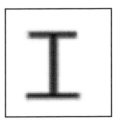

Meaning:
Very bad sign.
You are caught, or you shall be caught before you know it.
This is the end of the road.
There are plenty of evidence and documentations against you.
Follow the advice of the "Adjacent Cards" right now!

⌘⌘⌘

131

Meaning of each card

H "Hah", pronounced Hahh or Heh.
H in English.
Numerical value: 8.

Meaning:

1. The problem you are currently facing will dissipate.
2. You are on a solid ground, continue what you are doing.
3. Your second wish will not be fulfilled.
4. Answering your first question: No, they did not tell you the truth.

Reading and explanation of the First Line up of H "Heh".
If you get these 2 cards on your Bakht reading table.

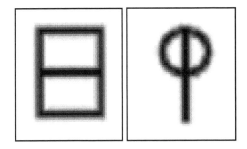

Meaning:
The problem you are currently facing will dissipate.
It was originally created by people you have trusted.
You are still on a solid ground, but you are concerned.
Get rid of fear and free your mind from negative thoughts.
Use common sense.
Now, you have to rebuild on a new foundation.

⌘ ⌘ ⌘

133

Reading and explanation of the First Line up of H "Heh".
If you get these 2 cards on your Bakht reading table.

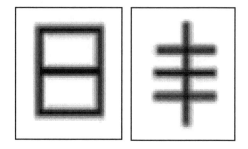

Meaning:
The problem you are currently facing will dissipate.
Your friends or partners did not tell you the truth. But you are very lucky, and you are going to know what was going behind your back. Your Double is watching over you.
You will win, but it is going to cost you.

⌘⌘⌘

Meaning of each card

T "Teh", pronounced Theh or Teth.
T in English.
Numerical value: 9.

Meaning:

1. Answering your first question: Yes, you will get it.
2. You are protected, but you are going to feel lonely and abandoned; this is a temporary feeling.
3. Good luck rides with you.
4. Answering your second question:
No, it is not a good relationship.

**Reading and explanation of the First Line up of T "Theh".
If you get these 2 cards on your Bakht reading table.**

Meaning:

You are protected by your Double, but you are going to feel lonely and abandoned; this is a temporary feeling.

No, it is not a good relationship.

This incident or event has happened before.

Unfortunately it is happening once again.

But because you are lucky and reasonable, you will deal with it successfully and end it permanently.

⌘⌘⌘

136

Meaning of each card.

Y "Yoda" pronounced Yo-Dah.
Y in English.
Numerical value: 10.

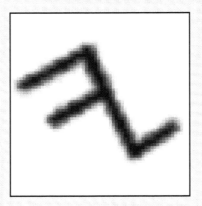

Meaning:

1. Avoid major decisions on Monday.
2. Tuesday, Thursday and Friday are your lucky days.
3. Your meticulous planning blends perfectly with an exquisite taste and an accentuated fantasy, yet not totally irrational. On the contrary, it adds originality and creates a special aura around you.
4. In your life, you will meet strong oppositions.
But with determination you will prevail.
5. Answering your first question:
Yes. It will happen, if you leave it alone. Don't try to interfere.
6. Answering your second question: Yes.
7. Answering your third question: Yes, if you act promptly.

Reading and explanation of the First Line up of Y "Yodah".
If you get these 2 cards on your Bakht reading table.

 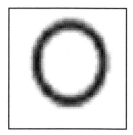

Meaning:
You will always attract people.
Your exquisite taste and an accentuated fantasy, make you a very special person. But these two gifts will irritate many and create envy and jealousy.
Many feel threatened by you, by your charm, and by your attractive personality. And those qualities infuriate competitors and those who do not know you well.
Present your cases or projects on Tuesday, Thursday and Friday, because they are your lucky days.
You are going to make it big time.
But when you reach the top of the ladder, be kind and grateful, and remember those you have left behind on your way up to ladder of success, especially those who put you there.
You have a spectacular future!

⌘⌘⌘

Meaning of each card

K "Kaf" pronounced Kaa'f.
K in English.
Numerical value: 11

Meaning:

1. Answer to your questions in general: Dominated by emotions.
Do not rush to conclusions.
The situation is not clear for the moment.
2. Your situation will improve. Good results will surface by the
end of the next cycle which ends on midnight of the first day of
the forthcoming week.
3. Not a good time for investment.
4. Answering your last question: You have the will, but not the
means. Wait for the forthcoming week to fully understand the
situation. Meanwhile, nothing bad or wrong will happen.

139

**Reading and explanation of the First Line up of K "Kaf".
If you get these 2 cards on your Bakht reading table.**

Meaning:
Do not fall prey to emotions.
In the past, and perhaps in the present, you have passed judgments based upon your emotions. This did not help.
In fact, those judgments and similar assumptions did not serve your interests, and you know it.
Now the cards are telling you to become more considerate and more reasonable.
The decision you are currently considering is not the most suitable one.
You should look at this situation from a different angle.
Consult the Bakht again on Tuesday night.

⌘ ⌘ ⌘

Meaning of each card

L "Lam" pronounced Lam and Lamda.
L in English.
Numerical value: 12.

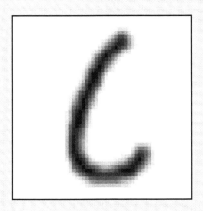

Meaning:

1. Answering your first question:
Yes, they might come after you.
2. Answering your second question:
Yes, stay quiet for now, but prepare plan b.
3. A major change will occur. Your partner will not interfere.
4. Answering your last question: Yes, you will find out. Some persons are involved, but by the end of this ordeal, they will side with you.

**Reading and explanation of the First Line up of L "Lam".
If you get these 2 cards on your Bakht reading table.**

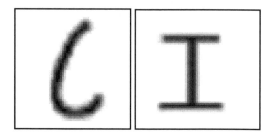

Meaning:
You will be facing a delicate financial situation in the near future, possibly in matters related to a partnership or a joint venture. This situation will not have a devastating effect on you, but could possibly jeopardize your financial stability.

In the future, pay closer attention to detail, and read the fine print.

You have been cheated, no doubt about it. But you are partially responsible, because you did not check all the facts.

If these sorts of situations happen again, based upon your poor judgment, you could lose everything you own, and end up in a dark alley.

The Bakht cannot prevent mishaps from happening.

To learn more about this, go to the section of cards line-up (Bakht Fast Reading).

⌘⌘⌘

Meaning of each card

M "Mim" pronounced Mem or Miim.
M in English.
Numerical value: 13.

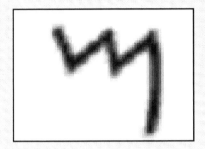

Meaning:

1. Your physical strength is bigger than your mental strength. But if you are patient, and you try again with determination and deep concentration, you will gain more mental power.

2. Tenderness and affection is the answer to your second question. Try diplomacy, but remain loyal and truthful.

3. Answering your second question:
No way out. Protect yourself.

4. Answering your third question: Before the end of the current month. But stay low key.

Reading and explanation of the First Line up of M "Mem".
If you get these 2 cards on your Bakht reading table.

Meaning:

Loyalty is a virtue.

Do you consider yourself a loyal person? Unconditionally? The cards are not so sure.

Manipulating people is self-destructive.

You have tried manipulation in the past, or perhaps used "White lies/tricks" to get what you want.

Maybe you are not yet ready to admit it.

A state of denial is not healthy.

You will be tempted again to use some tricks on others. It is not going to work anymore.

Within a few weeks, you are going to experience some financial difficulties. Reconsider your decision, and revise your plan.

Possibly you are going to feel confused about a new relationship. But your situation will improve, and good results will surface by the end of the next cycle which ends on midnight of the first day of the forthcoming week.

⌘⌘⌘

Meaning of each card

N "Nun" pronounced Noon.
N in English.
Numerical value: 14

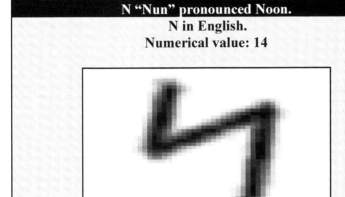

Meaning:

1. Answering your first question:
It happened before. It will happen again.
2. You have an opportunity to increase your income, but do change your location.
Or stay where you are and ask for a second opinion.
3. Answering your second question: You will see it right before your eyes.
4. General situation: You will have two choices. Act promptly.

**Reading and explanation of the First Line up of N "Nun".
If you get these 2 cards on your Bakht reading table.**

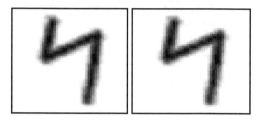

Meaning:
If you get these two cards, close the Bakht reading.

⌘ ⌘ ⌘

Meaning of each card

S "Samekh", pronounced Sa-Mekh.
S in English.
Numerical value: 15.

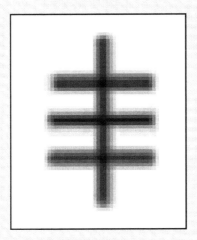

Meaning:

1. You are so lucky. Your Double is watching over you.
2. Answering your first question: Give them another chance.
3. Answering your second question: Yes.
4. Answering your third question: You will win, but it is going to cost you financially.
5. General situation:
You will never run out of luck. However, some financial losses are inevitable.
Your lucky days are Tuesday, Thursday and Sunday.

147

**Reading and explanation of the First Line up of S "Samekh".
If you get these 2 cards on your Bakht reading table.**

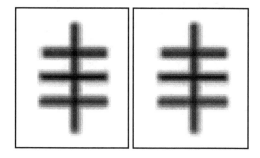

Meaning:
You were born lucky.
Adjust your spending habit.
Your Double is watching over you.

⌘ ⌘ ⌘

Reading and explanation of the Second Line up of S "Samekh".
If you get these 2 cards on your Bakht reading table.

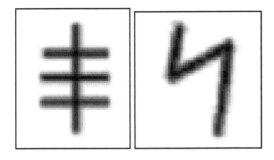

Meaning:
If you get these two cards, close the Bakht reading.

⌘ ⌘ ⌘

Reading and explanation of the Third Line up of S "Samekh".
If you get these 3 cards on your Bakht reading table.

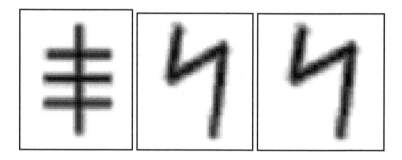

Meaning:

If you get these two cards, close the Bakht reading.

⌘ ⌘ ⌘

Meaning of each card

Ay'n "," pronounced Eye'n.

No corresponding letter or symbol in English, or in any other known language on Earth.

Note: In the Ana'kh, it is represented by a comma, standing for the continuum of an un-interrupted time, a non-linear time.

Numerical value: 16.

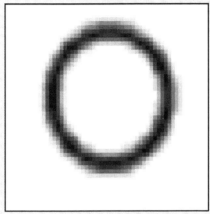

Meaning:

1. Answering your first question:

It is neither a good time nor a good location.

2. Answering your second question: Not this time.

3. Answering your third question:

You will get a positive answer. You will get help, but only for a short time. Others are going to change their mind, therefore, move fast, and reconsider what you thought about when you first learned about possible obstacles.

4. General situation: The current situation is not bright. Remain determined and strong. For the moment, time is not on your side, unless you compromise. You will know the outcome very soon.

Reading and explanation of the First Line up of Ayn "Eye of the Supreme Knowledge".
If you get these 2 cards on your Bakht reading table.

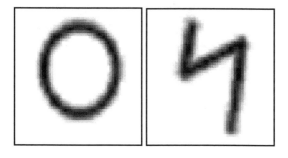

Meaning:
It would be a very bad idea to relocate now.

⌘ ⌘ ⌘

Reading and explanation of the Second Line up of Ayn "Eye of the Supreme Knowledge".
If you get these 2 cards on your Bakht reading table.

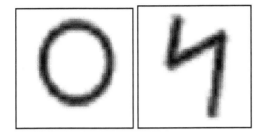

Meaning:
If you get these two cards, close the Bakht reading.

⌘ ⌘ ⌘

Reading and explanation of the Third Line up of Ayn "Eye of the Supreme Knowledge".
If you get these 3 cards on your Bakht reading table.

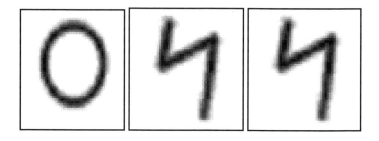

Meaning:
If you get these three cards, close the Bakht reading.

⌘⌘⌘

Meaning of each card

Q "Koph", pronounced Kop'fh.
Q in English.
Numerical value: 17.

Meaning:

1. Common sense. Precaution.
2. The opposite sex is your best ally.
3. Longevity is a part of your life scenario.
4. Answering your first question:
Evolution is rising. New prospects. Things will manifest.
5. Answering your second question:
You are still hesitant. Get rid of fear and free your mind from negative thoughts. Yes, it will come true, but first, repair the damages.
6. Answering your third question: You will prevail, if you take full control.
7. Answering your last question: You have caused damages. Admit guilt and rebuild on a new foundation.

Reading and explanation of the First Line up of Q "Koph"
If you get these 2 cards on your Bakht reading table.

Meaning:
You are going to have a long and healthy life.
The opposite sex is your best ally.
The opposite sex is also a stage for minor confrontations.
You attract women who argue a lot.

⌘⌘⌘

Meaning of each card

R "Resh" pronounced Reshh.
R in English.
Numerical value: 18.

Meaning:

1. You are candidate to play a major role in your field, and to leave a huge mark in this area.

2. You are going to face strong opposition in your most important projects. Such opposition will come from the opposite sex. And it will occur on the job, or where you work, such as an office, an organization, and even during a delegation and/a public speech. But you will be able to convince others and eliminate that opposition if this happens on these days: Tuesday, Thursday and Friday.

3. Monday is not a lucky day for you.

4. Answering your first question. Yes, for the moment.

5. Answering your second question: Yes again, but avoid arguments.

6. Answering your third question: No, put it behind you.

Reading and explanation of the First Line up of R "Resh".
If you get these 2 cards on your Bakht reading table.

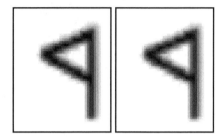

Meaning:
You are candidate to play a major role in your field, and to leave a huge mark in this area.
You will always face opposition, if your presentations are solely based on a surprise strategy. This could be your trademark.
You are not a favorite among colleagues at work.
But you are going to succeed no matter how, and no matter what, in almost everything you do.
Your lucky days are: Tuesday, Thursday and Friday.

⌘ ⌘ ⌘

Meaning of each card

Sh "Shin" pronounced S'hiin.
Sh in English.
Numerical value: 19.

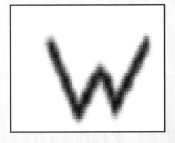

Meaning:
1. The possibilities are endless.
2. Confusion dominates. Do not relinquish your persistence.
3. The surroundings outside your work place is healthy.
4. Answering your first question:
You will get a good introduction. This will ease up the situation. Keep your secrets deep in your chest.
5. Answering your second question:
Yes. There is a negative influence at work It could spread to your entourage and habitat. Block the negative vibes.
6. Answering your second question: Not now. Try again.
7. Answering your third question: Accept what was proposed.
But ask an experienced and trusted friend to review the matter with you.
General situation: The situation will improve.
Be patient. Refresh your thoughts.

**Reading and explanation of the First Line up of Sh "Shin".
If you get these 2 cards on your Bakht reading table.**

Meaning:

The possibilities are endless, but you are going to have two major deceptions and spectacular success in your life.

For a short time, you will suffer from poor health, that could halt your entrepreneurial spirit, but you are going to recover fast, and pursue a brilliant career.

You are going to meet some very important people in your life.

You will gain their trust, confidence and support.

There is a negative influence at your work place.

It could spread to your entourage and habitat. Block the negative vibes.

⌘ ⌘ ⌘

160

Meaning of each card

Ni "Nihaya", pronounced Nee-Ha-Yah.
No corresponding letter in English.
Numerical value: 20.

Meaning:

1. Power of persuasion. Strong personality.
2. Your creativity and/or intelligence creates envy and jealousy among peers and associates. You should always consider more than one plan of action. Get your plan a, and your plan b handy.
3. Answering your first question: Not a very pleasant surprise.
4. Answering your second question: Yes. Keep it for yourself.
5. Answering your third question: No. This is the only solution.
General situation: Success. Many challenges.
You are fearless, but do not let your self-confidence disorient your decisions.

161

Reading and explanation of the First Line up of "Nihaya"
If you get these 2 cards on your Bakht reading table.

Meaning:
Your creativity and/or intelligence creates envy and jealousy among peers and associates.
You should always consider more than one plan of action.
Get your plan a, and your plan b handy.
You will have a great professional success.
But you will face many obstacles and enormous challenges.
You will triumph.

⌘⌘⌘

⌘ The Five Adjacent Cards⌘ ⌘

The Five Adjacent Cards are extremely important in the Bakht Dirasaat. They are usually used to reverse bad luck.

- ❖ E "Eh" Card.
- ❖ U "Uu" Card.
- ❖ I "Ii" Card.
- ❖ O "O" Card.
- ❖ P "P" Card.

163

⌘ The Five Adjacent Cards⌘ ⌘

The Five Adjacent Cards.

The following five cards are to be solely used in a second and a third reading, never before. Disregard them, if they do appear in a first Bakht reading. Further information and guidance are provided in book 2 of this series.

In a second reading:
E "Eh".
Pronunciation: Eh.
Numerical value: 21.

In a second reading:
U "Uu".
Pronunciation: Yu
Numerical value: 22.

In a third reading:
I "Ii".
Pronunciation: Ee.
Numerical value: 23.

In a third reading:
O "O".

Pronunciation: Ow
Numerical value: 24.

In a third reading:
P "P".
Pronunciation: Pef, Pt.
Numerical value: 25.

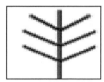

Note:

In volume 2, you will read about the technique of reversing bad luck, and the best days to use such techniques to block all negative vibes addressed toward you.

These vibes are not necessarily caused by others.

In many instances, you are the source of these bad vibrations.

And ironically, you are never aware of it.

In volume 2, I will show you how to block or get rid of these negative vibes, and how to project a mental shield of protection around your body.

⌘ ⌘ ⌘

CONTINUES IN PART 2 (Vol. 2)

NOTES

- Transcripts of what the Aliens, Extraterrestrials and Intraterrestrials Told our Governments.
- Mind-Bending Black Operations, Weapons Systems and Experiments by Extraterrestrials, Grays and Governments.
- Learn how to speak the Anunnaki Language
- The Grays, Alien Abductions and Genetic Creation of Humans Hybrids Race: Secret US Extraterrestrial Operations. Hybrids Habitats and Way of Life.
- The German UFOs, Extraterrestrials Messages and the Supernatural
- The Essential Maximillien de Lafayette. The Official Anunnaki Ulema Textbook for the Teacher and the Student. 2 volumes
- Inside the extraordinary world of the Anunnaki and Anunnaki Ulema: What I saw, what I learned, and what I can teach you.
- Anunnaki Genetic Creation of the Human Races, Demons and Spirits. How God was invented by the Egyptians, Sumerians, Phoenicians and Hebrews.
- When Heaven Calls You: Connection with the Afterlife, Spirits, 4th Dimension, 5th Dimension, Higher-Self, Astral Body, Parallel Dimensions and the Future
- Activation of the Conduit and the Supersymetric Mind. Beyond the Third Eye and Toward the Oneness.
- Baalbeck: The Anunnaki City and Afrit Underground.
- Description, Translation, and Explanation of Babylonian, Sumerian, Akkadian, Assyrian, Ugaritic,

Anunnaki and Phoenician Cylinder Seals, Slabs, Tablets and Inscriptions.
- The Complete Anunnaki Ulema Tarot Deck. Lessons And Techniques To See Your Future.
- Anunnaki Chronology and their Remnants on Earth From 1,250,000 B.C. to the Present Day.
- De Lafayette Mega Encyclopedia of Anunnaki, Ulema-Anunnaki, their Offspring, their Remnants and Extraterrestrial Civilization on Earth.
- 2022 Anunnaki Code: End of the World and their Return to Earth. Ulema Book of Parallel Dimension, Extraterrestrials and Akashic Records
- Ulema Secret Teachings on Anunnaki, Extraterrestrials, UFOs, Alien Civilizations and How to Acquire Paranormal Powers.

*** *** ***

New Books by
Maximillien de Lafayette
Available at amazon.com and lulu.com

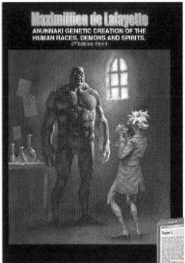 

Cover of Vol. 1   Cover of Vol. 2

Anunnaki Genetic Creation of the Human Races, Demons and Spirits. 5th Edition. (In 2 Volumes)

The book IS EXPLOSIVE and AUTHORITATIVE! It contains hundreds of photographs, illustrations, maps, sketches and inscriptions, tablets and slabs translated from Sumerian and Akkadian by the author, a world authority on ancient languages and Anunnaki.

5,000 year old tablets demonstrated that WE ARE NOT CREATED BY THE GOD OF THE BIBLE. We were genetically created by the Anunnaki. This book has all the proofs to convince you once for good! The Anunnaki created the human race, God, Gods, angels, spirits and demons before the dawn of the history of Man. Don't be offended, GOD was created by the Egyptian priests, and the Mesopotamian myths/epics. And organized religions are cashing on it!

The extraterrestrials created many species and different human races here on planet Earth. But there are other early human beings who were created in space, and on other planets, and like the very small and very tall species, they were not part of the evolutionary process of the modern human beings. In total, 36 (some say 46) different human and quasi-human species lived on planet Earth in many regions of the globe. And none of them were created by the "God" we know and worship. After all, they did not look like humans, and if we have to believe that humans were created in the image of "God", as Judaism, Christianity and Islam tell us, then, most certainly those early 36 different species who looked like ferocious beasts, were not made in the image of "God".

The Anunnaki, Igigi and other extraterrestrial civilizations created several models of early human beings, Negative entities, reptilians, Djinns, Afrit, evil-birds, and demons which live in the lower sphere/zone (Alternate dimension), and on Earth

Also you will read about:

Names of the Anunnaki gods and goddesses who created the first humans, and the genetic creation of the human race

The Igigi who created the first quasi human/robots

The Akkadian text on the creation of Man

Anunnaki geneticists who developed DNA sequences, and altered the genes of hybrids

The early human forms

The Earth-made human creatures

The Space-made human creatures

Metabolism and the oceans-made human creatures

Evolution of the extraterrestrials and the human races

Negative entities, reptilians, Djinns, Afrit, evil-birds, and demons which live in the lower sphere/zone (Alternate dimension), and on Earth

Anamidra explains the creation of Man from cosmic clay

Copies of the universe, including copies of ourselves, and Earth in other dimensions

Dual nature of humans, before they were separated genetically

"Grays": Intraterrestrial non-human

How the Anunnaki created us genetically in their laboratories.

*** *** ***

172

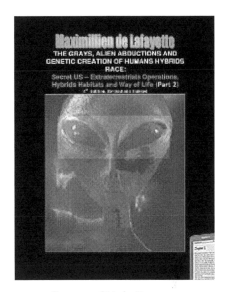

Cover of Vol. 1   Cover of Vol. 2

The Grays, Alien Abductions and Genetic Creation of Humans
Hybrids Race: Secret US - Extraterrestrials Operations.
Hybrids Habitats and Way of Life.4th Edition, (Aliens and
hybrids among us) In 2 Volumes

The book includes:
1.Description of the hybrids' habitat.
2.Hybrids underground/underwater communities.
3.Their bedrooms, beds, toys, dining rooms, food, and eating habits.
4.Hybrids' three distinct groups/categories.
5.Hybrids placed for adoption.
6.The Grays fetuses' room, and how they genetically create a human-
hybrid race.
7.Intraterrestrial Grays and their abductees: Rapports, relationship
and abductees' accounts.
8.The future of the human race and the global change.
9.Weather/Climate weapons system, invented by the military and
Grays.
10.HAARP.
11.Weapon system used to suck up the oxygen from the air we
breathe.
12.Aliens-US frightening military technology.
13.Extraterrestrials-US joint black operations.
14.The device used to create a holographic projection

173

15.Project Serpo, Zeta Reticuli, and Stargate
16. Scenes from the future, as projected by the Grays on holographic screens.
17.Holographic zooming at some intelligence agencies.
18.How the aliens can move American cities, like New York to another place or make them disappear?
19.How the aliens cured an abductee a lung cancer.
20.US military scientists and the Corridor Plasma
21.Massive underwater bases and joint human-alien operations.
22.The American military has successfully sent six men through the vortex, to another dimension.
23.Aliens/Grays-US Dulce Base war, and the killing of 66 American soldiers.
24.Holographic pictures showing the entire sequence of the Roswell crash.
25.The aliens Radio plasma belt around earth to isolate earth from the universe.
26.Descritpion of the Dulce underground base, and the living quarters of aliens inside the base.
27.Genetic labs that created half human/ half animals.
28.And much much more.

*** *** ***

WHEN THE GODS DESCENDED ON EARTH: The Phoenicians-Extraterrestrials Link (2 Volumes in paperback)

Cover of Vol. 1   Cover of Vol. 2

It includes hundreds of photos and illustrations. An exposé based upon the history, geography, religion, theology, languages, epistemology, etymology, archeology, time-table and chronology, philosophy, sociology of the Phoenicians and ancient civilizations of the Near East, Middle East, Anatolia, the Bible, and Kira'at of the Anunnaki Ulema to prove that the Extraterrestrial Gods descended on Phoenicia and how the Anunnaki shaped our history, destiny and future. The author discusses these topics in the book, and provides solid evidence pertaining to the early Phoenicians' link to the Extraterrestrial Gods and Ancient Aliens who descended first on Phoenicia, as well as the primordial influence the early Phoenicians had on the creation of the concept of God, Judaism, and Christianity.

| Cover of Vol. 1 | Cover of Vol. 2 |

YEAR 2022. Anunnaki Code: End Of The World And Their Return To Earth. (Return of the Extraterrestrial Gods) In 2 Parts

Most of the material of this book has been learned from sources that are totally out of reach for the average reader, and ufology's milieu. Some was hidden in the archives of museums, some written on tablets that have never been translated before, and some of it is oral knowledge that have never been given to a Westerner before. The author, Maximillien de Lafayette, have been so fortunate as to study with those who are the guardians of this knowledge in the East. This is the first time he is making use of this depot of knowledge, and we are very lucky to have access to it. The subjects introduced in this book are explosive. Most important is the fact that it reveals the potential return of the Anunnaki in 2022, and the most frightening transformation that it would bring to the earth. If this is going to happen, a huge number of the people on earth, those grossly contaminated by Grays' DNA, will be annihilated. You know who they are - the child murderers, the rapists, those who torture, those who abuse, etc. Yes, we all know who they are. But the Anunnaki, who have no false sentimentality at all, will not tolerate even a medium level contamination. Unless they do their best to clean themselves

176

during the grace period of the next eleven years, those of mid level contamination will also be destroyed. Those who would manage to clean themselves to a certain degree may possibly (but without any guarantee) be able to escape the burning, smoking earth through special portals, called Ba'abs. Only those who are naturally uncontaminated and those who managed to clean themselves completely will be taken up through an antimatter bubble, with the animals and certain important buildings and inanimate art and culture objects, and kept safe until the earth would be clean again. Such a scenario is, to say the least, disconcerting.

Even if you are not sure whether you are a believer or not, you should certainly consider the possibilities - and the book teaches you exactly how to save yourself. For those who are interested in the use of esoteric codes, they are here to learn from. Each term will teach you how to use it for your benefit, how to apply it not only to your spiritual growth, but to your business, relationships, and daily life.

You will learn how to interpret the codes in many ancient languages, how to build a physical amulet/code that will protect certain aspects of your life, and how to develop your psychic and extrasensory powers by simply using these codes.

You will learn how the Anunnaki were our original creators, who else tempered with our genetic materials, and how God factors into all this. Religion, true and false, will be explored. Jesus, who never really died on the Cross, will be shown as a historical figure, with his wife, Mary Magdalene, with whom he escaped to ancient Marseille. Who were Adam and Eve? Who was the Serpent? How do the gods of Sumer signify to us?

You will be asked to consider the old theory, now discarded, that the Anunnaki came here to mine gold. You will meet the earliest extraterrestrial-human civilization, and no, it was not Sumer. It was, believe it or not, Phoenicia! You will learn many secrets about the Anunnaki themselves - such as their extrasensory

powers, their deep knowledge of genetics and science, and their unbelievably long lifespan.

Who is their God?

What kind of social classes they have?

What spiritual principles do they exercise?

And most important, what is their 2022 plan for humanity after the apocalyptic cleansing of the earth.

LEARN HOW TO SPEAK THE ANUNNAKI LANGUAGE:
Dictionary, Vocabulary, Conversation

Including etymology, epistemology, the study and linguistic investigation of the derivation and origin of the ancient Middle and Near East languages, Semitic and non-Semitic languages and dialects, including, but not limited to Old Babylonian, Akkadian, Sumerian, Assyrian, Chaldean, Aramaic, Phoenician, Ugaritic, Hebrew, Hittite, Arabic, etc.

Comparison with Akkadian, Sumerian, Assyrian, Arabic, Hebrew, Aramaic, Phoenician, Chaldean, Hittite, Ugaritic, Babylonian. A WORLD PREMIERE EVENT.

For the first time in philology's history, and chronicles of civilizations of the ancient world, Maximillien de Lafayette, a world renowned expert linguist (Ancient Languages) provides us with the first lexicon/thesaurus/dictionary of the Anunnaki and Ulemite languages. This book is a treasure. It consists of a set of 4 volumes. The last volume focuses on Anunnaki and Igigi language conversation. And YES you will be able to speak their terrestrial and extraterrestrials languages as spoken on Earth and their planet.

This unique work consists of definitions of words, etymology, epistemology, the study and linguistic investigation of the derivation and origin of the ancient Middle and Near East languages, Semitic and non-Semitic languages and dialects, including, but not limited to Old

Babylonian, Akkadian, Sumerian, Assyrian, Chaldean, Aramaic, Phoenician, Ugaritic, Hebrew, Hittite, Arabic, etc.

Ana'kh is the language of the Anunnaki who descended on ancient Turkey, Mesopotamia, and Phoenicia according to the Ulema. It is of an extraterrestrial origin. Ulema Al Bakr stated that it was used by early the human beings who lived in ancient Anatolia, on the Island of Arwad, in Tyre, Sidon, Byblos, Ugarit, Amrit, and Mu. He added that from the Ana'kh derived the primitive languages of the Near East and the Middle East. Ana'kh was never made public.

It remained a secret language known only to the Ulema, and later on to the Allamah. It sounds Semitic, because of its phonetics. But it is "not Semitic at all", said Ulema Ghandar Gupta.

It has no grammar, but it has an extremely rich vocabulary and an abundance of metaphoric expressions.

A considerable number of Akkadian and Sumerian words that appeared in the Sumerian/Akkadian/Chaldean Epic of Creation and the Bible derived from Ana'kh.

Around 569 A.D., a group of Ulema (Munawareen) in the Near East (Non-Islamic scholars) compiled an extensive list of Ana'kh words and phrases. In 625, A.D., two leading figures of the Ulema brotherhood wrote the Book of Rama-Dosh; a compilation of Ana'kh terminology, a lexicon, and Kiraats (Readings).

Ulema AL Bakr stated that the Ulema are not member of a religious group. They are neither Muslim nor members of any organized religion. In fact, they were persecuted by the companions of the Prophet Muhammad, and were expelled from the Arab Peninsula. They found refuge in Cyprus and Marseille. But the honorable Ulema was quick to point out that the early Sufi masters, poets and Sufi trance dancers were Ulema. He added that Ulema should not be confused with the Islamic Ulema who teach Islamic law, or with the Allamah who were the leading Islamic figures of science and letters in medieval times.

Farid Tayarah, an Ulema himself, and a former head of a Masonic Lodge stated that the Ana'kh was used during Masonic sessions and services. He added that a considerable number of Masonic words and expressions are pure Ana'kh, especially those words referring to levels and degrees in Freemasonry, and initiation ceremonies.

Many of the original words of this language, as well as numerous linguistic derivations are included in this book.

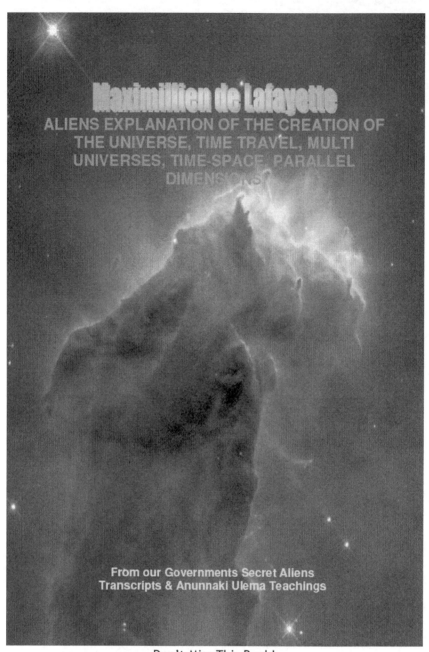

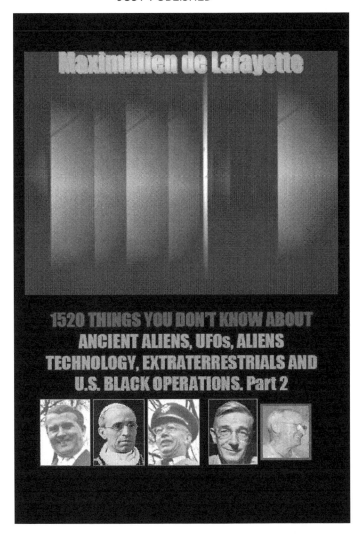

1520 Things You Don't Know about Ancient Aliens, UFOs, Aliens Technology, Extraterrestrials and U.S. Black Operations. Part 2

Part 2 (Final volume). The 2 volumes are available in paperback at lulu.com

The importance of this groundbreaking book resides in the originality of its material and world-premiere information on UFOs, USOs, extraterrestrials, intraterrestrials, aliens, alien technology, U.S. black operations and aliens multiple universes, not readily available elsewhere, and covering the most important events and findings in the history of modern ufology and the study of alien civilization, parallel universes, and multiple dimensions, as DIRECTLY explained to us by the extraterrestrials we met with since 1947.

Nowhere, in any published book, on websites, in conferences and other published material, you will ever find the information, data, briefings and reports provided in this book. For instance (Information and reports never revealed before or known to ufologists and the general public):

In this volume:

1. The Grays and the BL-rm3
2. 4 UFOs crashes on record
3. Human bodies' parts were found inside an alien spacecraft
4. Excerpts from the Aliens Transcripts of our meetings with extraterrestrials and intraterrestrials in 1947 and 1948
5. Scientist and Nobel Prize winner, Dr. Francis Crick wrote: "The astonishing hypothesis is, that there is no soul." This is exactly what the aliens told the military.
6. What the aliens told us about Jesus, the disciples, the four Biblee and the Gnostics.
7. Aliens Rewinding Time Technology
8. Translation Signals Box (TSB): A machine the aliens gave us, which allowed us to respond to their communications and messages
9. CTF (Transmission Channel): A device used by military scientists to receive messages from aliens
10. The Web: A network of underwater channels linking together intraterrestrial communities
11. VCP: Vortex Tunnel Weapon System
12. The military has successfully sent some of its personnel through a vortex tunnel to another dimension, and successfully, they were brought back
13. Aliens Spinning Mobile Satellite" (SMS): The mode of transportation down the underwater bases
14. Corridor Plasma and the Vacuum Tunnel: Underwater cold plasma tunnel used by the intraterrestrials (The Grays) to navigate underwater
15. Bioelectric extraterrestrial robots "B.E.R": Human-like robots capable of acting like human beings

16. Aliens zooming into the past and jumping into the future
17. BCB: The Aliens Compressor Machine
18. List of names of scientists who collaborated with aliens and/or worked on alien reverse engineering
19. Major discoveries based on alien technology
20. Non-disclosure policy by Catholic archbishops and secret committees. (Their names and role)
21. On Presidents Truman, Eisenhower, Nixon and Bush Sr. knowledge of and involvement with the alien phenomenon.
22. The shipped aliens' dead bodies to Walter Reed Hospital

DO NOT MISS THESE TWO BOOKS ON GERMAN UFOS, MYSTICISM
AND OCCULT IN NAZI GERMANY
**GERMAN UFOS: MODELS & CATEGORIES, ENGINEERS &
SCIENTISTS, EXTRATERRESTRIALO MESSAGES,
SUPERNATURAL, LADIES OF THE VRIL, U.S. LINK**

Cover of Volume 1

184

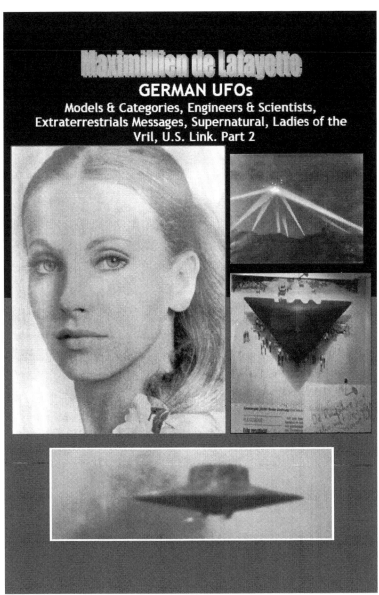

Cover of Volume 2

INDEX

INDEX

A

A…65,67,68
Aa-kim-lu…20
Abekir…20
Abharu-Ak-Sha…20
A.D., 65…21
A.D., 1365…22
Afrit…21,33
Akkadian…21,25
Akkadian/Sumerian clay
    tablets…83
Al Baydani, Cheik …22
Al Donia, Ilmu …21,22,34
Alchemists…19
Al Moustakbal, Dirasat…22
Alef…89
Alexander the Great…99
Alshich, Hakadosh…20
Alter the future…79,84
Alter the present…79
Anah-Taba.Ru…20
Ana'kh…21,25,53,61,67,68,97
    Proto Ugaritic…21,61,65,67
    Terminology…31
    Your name
    in…53,56,61,65,67
Anda-Barikha…20
Anna.Ki…19
Anu.Na.Ki…19,33,44,50,51,56
    ,61,83,84,186
    Sinhars…20
    Ulema Anunnaki…20,44
Arab scholars…21
Arabic language…21

Arabic Peninsula…21
Arabic tradition…55
Archamides…20
Aruru…83
Arwah…21,33
Ashraaf…43
Atmospheric conditions…44
Awareness…83
Ayn…66,92

B

B…65
Baal-Shamroutiim…20,33
Ba-khaat…20,33
Babylonian, old…21,25
Bach…84
Badri, Ulema…85
Bakhaati…21,33
Bakht…50,73,83
    Cards…73
    Kiraat…19
    Manuscript…21
    Meaning of…21
    Reading the…21,51,74,84
    Study of…19
    Practiced by…19,20,
    Techniques of …2
    Terminology of…33
Bakht Haya.Ti…33,45
B.C., 7,500…21
Behavior, good…84
Ben Shmuel Abulafia,
    Avraham…20
Ben Yacob, Master…22
Ben Zvi, Mordachai …22
Bet…89

189

192

M

195

CONTINUES IN PART 2 (Vol. 2)

Published by
Times Square Press

Printed in the United States of America

Made in the USA
Middletown, DE
16 August 2015